'AN EVENING C‎‎‎‎‎‎

A Th‎‎‎‎‎
the Histc

in DARSHAM

A Chronicle of a Suffolk Church

by

Olive Reeve & Richard Ginn

2nd Edition

© Copyright Olive D. Reeve 1999
© Copyright Richard J. Ginn 1999
© Copyright Ronald Reeve 2014.

Published by:
The Darsham Parochial Church Council
Sold in aid of All Saints' Church Fabric Fund

This edition published in 2014. Printed by Leiston Press. 01728 833003.

ISBN 978-0-9536592-4-1

All rights reserved. No part of this publication may be reproduced, stored in or introduced into a retrieval system, or transmitted, in any form or by any means (electronical, mechanical, photocopying, recording or otherwise), without prior permission of both the copyright owners and the publishers of this book.

Acknowledgements:

Bodleian Library
British Library
Cambridge University Library
Lambeth Palace Library
Norfolk Record Office
Public Record Office, Kew
Suffolk Library Service
Suffolk Record Office
East Anglian Daily Times
& Eastern Counties Newspapers Ltd.
Mrs Elizabeth Alexander
Mrs Sara Low
Andrew Campbell

Original edition printed in 2000 by:
Suffolk Design & Print.

Cover Photo: *A rooftop view of the Church from Ivy Cottages.*

Preface to the Second Edition
by Revd. Canon Richard Ginn

The enthusiasm which greeted the first edition of this book took the authors by surprise. We were delighted that the print-run was soon exhausted and then amazed at the way that copies attracted fierce competition as they came on the second-hand market.

The need for this second edition demonstrates the fact that a parish Church is a special place to be cherished. Our Church in Darsham carries resonances for us by which it acts as the guardian of the identity of the village and anchors us in the context of the centuries through which it has stood.

Local history is our history; it is the history of everyone who has participated in our village. This little book has to be taken with its two companion volumes, 'The Watch that Ends the Night' and 'Before the Rising Sun'. Together they form a new bench-mark in local history, and are a remarkable testimony to the painstaking work of the late Olive Reeve in shaping meaningful patterns of evidence out of the dust of past ages.

These three volumes depict the lives of the people of Darsham over the centuries and is a testament to them and their way of life. It is to be hoped that our village will continue to be marked by compassion, mutual care and public worship in the years to come.

Preface to the First Edition.
by Revd. Richard Ginn

Mrs Olive Reeve has been the Local History Recorder at Darsham for 16 years. As she has searched out various items of personal interest, it became apparent that she was beginning to assemble a history of the village. Such is the diligence of her research, aided and abetted by her husband, that the project has more or less taken over a room of their house.

As the millennium has approached, the conviction has grown that there is a story to tell. The problem was to find a theme that would enable the story to emerge. Mrs Reeve suggested that an account of the Parish Church in Darsham would get the most out of the mass of data available. So we set to work. A great deal of information has had to be omitted so that the story does not become choked with detail. My contribution has been to turn a great many particles of information into a connected account. I must thank Andrew Campbell, currently both organist and PCC Secretary, for reading the drafts and suggesting many felicities of phrasing. Thanks must also be rendered to the anonymous donor who has paid for the first printing of this book.

It has been very interesting to reflect on the way that questions have arisen as we have prepared this text. Answers have only emerged because of the extent of the sources that Mrs Reeve has marshalled in Record Offices. Of course there will be gaps, but when sufficient extra information is forthcoming there can always be another edition! There may be errors, but we trust that these will be

Preface

understood as having only arisen from the best of intentions.

History is meant to be a tool of enlightenment - and perhaps through the pages of this work we can more readily appreciate the village of today by recognising the achievements of those who have gone before us. We have to learn from history. So often, we see the suffering that arises when history is ignored and the same cycles of mistakes are repeated. At least in Darsham we can discover something of the identity of our community as we see patterns in the myriad details that constitute our history. And as we find the identity of our village as it is expressed over a thousand years, so we may have a clearer sense of what we cherish in this place and in one another.

This book is dedicated to the future of the Church in Darsham, in gratitude for the dedication of all those who have gone before.

> O God our help in ages past,
> Our hope for years to come,
> Our shelter from the stormy blast,
> And our eternal home;
>
> A thousand ages in thy sight
> Are like *an evening gone*,
> Short as the watch that ends the night
> Before the rising sun.

Psalm 90 - verses by Isaac Watts

CONTENTS

Introduction. 1

Chapter 1 - The Mediaeval Church. 3

Chapter 2 - The Reformation. 10

Chapter 3 - Late Tudors & Early Stuarts. 18

Chapter 4 - Civil War & Restoration. 23

Chapter 5 - The Eighteenth Century. 32

Chapter 6 - The Nineteenth Century. 41

Chapter 7 - The Twentieth Century. 59

Chapter 8 - Conclusion. 82

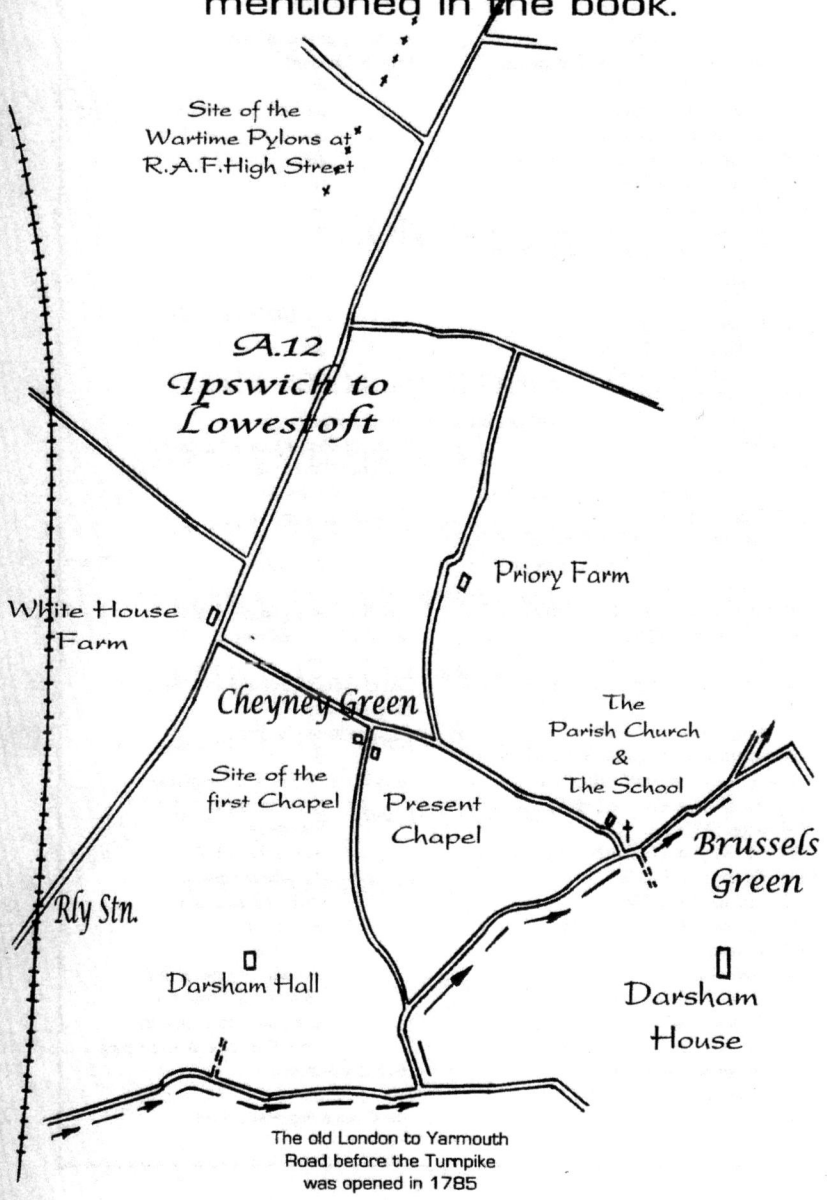

DARSHAM VICARS — 1311 to date

	Patron
1311 - Robert de BANHAM	Prior & Convent of Thetford
1330 - William RYKEDOUN	
1349 - William SUCLING	Maria, Countess of Norfolk
1351 - John Le SPENCER de Cretingham	Prior of Thetford
1361 - Nicholas AWNSEL	do
1364 - William AUNCELL	do
1395 - Galfredus HAUKE	do
1399 - Alexander de WEST WALTON	do
? - John COKYSSON	do
1409 - William COLBY	do
1432 - William MARSHALL	do
1432 - John BROMPTON or BRAMPTON	do
1455 - Michael GOSSE	do
? - Jac FOWLYSS	do
1474 - Roger WARNER	do
1504 - William WYNSTON	do
1520 - William BURNHAM	do
1532 - John SPENCER	do

1536 - 1540 Dissolution of the Monasteries.

1555 - John TORRE	Exors. of Thos. Duke of Norfolk
1564 - Richard HALL	Thomas Duke of Norfolk
1575 - Laurance MANWARING als. MOORE	Wm.Dix & another
1581 - Henry GRAY	Edward Hemyng Esq.
1583 - Nicholas WYLDY or WIDNEY or WIDLY	do
1616 - John EACHARD (*bur.Darsham 1647*)	Thomas Bedingfield
c.1647 - Samuel GOLBY	
1683 - Thomas WARREN (*prev. the Curate*)	Elizabeth Bedingfield — widow
1706 - John EDWARDS (*Curate 1708/9*)	Sir John Rous 2nd bart.
1720 - Benjamin TAYLOR	
1748 - Robert BUXTON (*married his Patron*)	Dame Lydia Rous (Widow of Sir Robt Rous 4th bart)
1775 - Michael Driver MEASE	Sir John Rous, 6th bart.
1789 - William KETT (*lived at Melton 1804-6*)	do
1832 - William Langstaff WEDDALL	John Rous - 1st Earl of Stradbroke
1851 - Thomas Rabbet MAYHEW	Hereafter the
1866 - John THORPE	Patronage
1889 - Christopher TENNANT M.A.,D.C.L.	was in the gift of
1928 - Edward J.GRANT	the subsequent
1932 - Thomas BENNETT	Earls of Stradbroke
1933 - Rowland W.MAITLAND	until 1971
1947 - Herbert RUGLYS	when the
1950 - Harry LEE	Church Commissioners
1952 - Ernest HAMMOND	decreed that Darsham
1953 - Canon PYKE	should become a Plurality
1954 - Charles Lansley WALLER	with Westleton & Dunwich
1971 - James S.LOVEJOY	Church Commissioners
1974 - Ian Cameron ROBINSON	Earl of Stradbroke
1985 - Richard GINN	The Church Patronage Trust

THE CHURCH IN DARSHAM

ALL SAINTS' CHURCH

Introduction

The Parish Church of All Saints' stands at the eastern end of The Street in Darsham, furthest away from the noise and bustle of the A.12 road that is still called the Turnpike by those who were born and brought up here. The turnpike was opened in 1785. Before that time, the main road from London to Great Yarmouth went past the church. It came up from Yoxford via the Westleton Road, turning along Low Road in Darsham and, leaving the church on its left, continued up past Brussels Green and onward via Hinton & Blythburgh.

Nowadays, standing at Church Corner we could be deceived by our immediate surroundings. At the junction of three roads, the church stands in the tree-lined churchyard surrounded by eight cottages. These are now privately owned, but originally they were part of the Darsham Town Trust, a local charity so old that its origins cannot be discovered. Rents from these properties in 1838, for example, provided income to defray the costs of church repairs, books and ornaments; the salary of the Sunday-schoolmaster, sexton and parish clerk; £4 to the

Introduction

Sunday school, and to the relief of the poor of the parish; all done with £27.13s.0d. Now it is difficult to appreciate just how old these cottages are, as their internal history is concealed behind more modern exteriors, so it is even more difficult to make a leap of the imagination and grasp the age of the site on which the church stands.

At the end of the twentieth century, we are used to the parish as an administrative unit. In former times the parish was made up of *manors*, which were basically farming units that varied in size, and which did not have to conform to parish boundaries. The other unit of administration was the *hundred*. Darsham belonged in the Hundred of Blything. Again, hundreds varied in size, and were first recorded in England in the time of King Edgar (959-975). The Blything Hundred was the largest grouping in Suffolk. The inhabitants of the hundred were collectively responsible for the maintenance of the peace. Until 1886, the hundred was liable for damage caused by rioters, and yes, there was a riot, as is revealed in the following pages.

Chapter One

The Mediaeval Church

A church has stood on this site for a thousand years. Certainly some of the present church dates from Norman times. It was rebuilt during the 15th & 16th century when it was one of fifteen churches in Suffolk under the care of the cluniac monks of Thetford Priory.

Darsham is mentioned in the Domesday Survey of 1086. In that compendium, Darsham is called Dersam, Diresham, and Dersham - all meaning the place of the deer. It is not difficult to see deer around the village today, though whether local people still catch them for venison is another matter.

Before the Norman Conquest, it is recorded that Darsham Church was held as part of a manor by a priest called Alwin. By 1086, this land was classified as 'Land of the King, Belonging to the Realm, which Roger Bigod keeps in Suffolk'. Roger Bigod had accompanied William in his invasion of 1066. In 1086, this Roger Bigod had substantial lands of his own in Suffolk, including land in Darsham, where his tenants were listed as including Ansketel the Priest, who was also credited with being Bigod's chaplain, and Wulfric the Deacon. Roger Bigod came from a French family, and by the time of the Domesday Survey he was the sheriff of Suffolk and Norfolk. He came to be the ancestor of the Earls of Norfolk.

At this time, the great monastery of Cluny in France was developing in power and significance. Cluny had been founded in 909, and set a high standard of monastic observance, which was adopted as a pattern for reform by other monasteries. At Cluny, there was a return to the strict Benedictine rule, stress on the cultivation of the personal spiritual life, but an emphasis on sharing in splendid and solemn worship with a corresponding reduction in manual labour. Attention was also paid to sound economic organisation. At the beginning of the twelfth century, the new abbey church at Cluny was the largest church in Europe (555 feet long). The Abbot of Cluny was St Hugh (1024-1109), and he became a personal friend of St Anselm, the theologian and philosopher, who was Archbishop of Canterbury from 1093 until his death in 1109. St Anselm had major differences with the king of England. He had to spend some years in exile and frequently visited Cluny. Hugh commended the Cluniacs in England to Anselm's protection - a favour he was pleased to grant. Meanwhile, various priories were established as outposts of the abbey at Cluny to support the mother house at Cluny and to share in its ideals. When Roger Bigod wanted to found Thetford, it was on Anselm's advice that he applied to Cluny, and so, in a way, the great Anselm made the connection between Darsham and Cluny.

The remains of Thetford Abbey
founded by Roger Bigod c.1104
to which he endowed land & the church in Darsham

A Cluniac Monk of Thetford Abbey
would have been Vicar of Darsham
from the rebuilding of the church
in the 14th century until the dissolution
of the monasteries about 1540

The Mediaeval Church

It may seem a long way from the enormous building at Cluny to a little church at Darsham, which at that time consisted of just part of the present chancel. Thetford Priory was founded in 1103-4, and after a false start, building began in 1107 just before Roger Bigod died. Building continued throughout the twelfth century. The huge endowment needed for the new priory was settled by the Bigod family and included their lands at Darsham, along with the church. The priory at Thetford became responsible for staffing the parish church. Those long forgotten links with Thetford Priory are remembered locally by the name 'Priory Farm'.

Thetford Priory expected to receive income from their lands in Darsham, but at the same time the priory was committed to the pastoral care of the villagers, and to share in the maintenance of the parish church. The accounts of the priory for the years 1482 until its dissolution in 1540 have survived, and expenses were regularly paid for repairs to the chancel and for strawing the church floor. In 1507/8 substantial repairs amounted to £3.15s.8d, and in 1525 repairs were 18s.2d. In 1536 it was recorded that three buttresses were built on to the chancel at a cost of £2.8s.0d after which the church was limed and re-thatched. The thatcher and his man were paid for 22 days work (presumably 11 days each) at a cost of 11s. plus the boarding of the two men for this time at a cost of 9s.2d. No trace remains of those buttresses because there have been later alterations to the chancel.

The Mediaeval Church

There survives a list of vicars appointed to Darsham from Thetford that reaches back to 1311. These priests were called vicars because they were put in post to represent the monastery, the word *vicar* technically meaning *substitute*. A vicar received the *small tithe* for his maintenance. This was the tithe of minor produce (lambs, chickens, etc.). The monastery received the *great tithe* (wheat, oats, etc.). The small tithes were usually difficult to collect, but a vicar would also have the benefit of glebe land that he could either cultivate himself or rent out.

Whilst monks were encouraged to do a measure of manual work, they would have been expected to spend a total of about eight hours each day conscientiously in church at services. However, a monk appointed as vicar to Darsham was a long way from Thetford and may have found competing claims on his time because the need to produce food was fairly pressing, especially given the great shortage of labour after the Black Death. Economic and spiritual demands were closely intertwined.

That terrible plague, the Black Death, almost certainly came to Darsham, as one vicar was appointed in 1349, probably replacing a plague victim, and then another was appointed in 1351 after the plague had abated, possibly a delayed appointment replacing another victim.

To us it may seem a strange mixture: a monk saying prayers in the little church in Latin, whilst the villagers lived at subsistence level and spoke in their own dialect. Most of

The Mediaeval Church

the services would not have been attended by the villagers, but they would have known that their priest was praying, and that would have been an important form of security. They needed the assurance that God knew about them, and cared about them, in a frightening world. When they went to see the host elevated at mass, they knew that God was amongst them.

At this time, the population of Darsham must have been very small. In the years after the Black Death of 1349, dozens of villages in East Anglia ceased to exist. It is quite surprising that out of the tiny numbers at Darsham we know of three men who went on to become parish priests elsewhere. Two men were monks at Leiston Abbey, and one succeeded the other as vicar at Theberton, marking an early point in our relationships with that village. Robert de Dersham became Vicar of Theberton in 1374, to be followed by John de Dersham in 1391. Another Darsham man, Geoffrey Symond, was Vicar of Lopham in Norfolk 1394-1404, then Rector of Bradwell in Suffolk 1404-1410, and probably also Vicar of St Mary-in-the-Marsh, Norwich, 1409-1410. He gave the present font to Darsham Church, and it is likely that the original font is preserved amongst the ruins of Sibton Abbey as a washing bowl.

About a hundred years after the time of the Black Death the economic life of the region began to recover. Darsham may have drawn some benefit from this, particularly as Dunwich had lost much of its economic importance. Trade went through the middle of Darsham, on the king's highway from

The Mediaeval Church

London to Great Yarmouth. There is an indication of rising local prosperity in that several legacies were given in wills between the years 1460 and 1505 towards building the church tower. It was a common feature of life in those days for individuals to leave bequests to the parish church; for example, the will of Roger Reve of 1540 left 'two bushels of wheat to the Church & Clerke of Darsham for tithes neglected'. Two brasses set in the nave floor bearing the names of Reve and Garard date from the years 1480-1540; another sign of local wealth that such symbols of prestige could be afforded. The oldest of the four bells, dedicated to St Thomas, dates from the period 1460-1500. The bell is a sign of the significance of the village at that time. The ringing of the bell had important social and spiritual functions in late mediaeval England. These have been summarised as being to praise God; call the people; toll for funerals; subdue thunderstorms; mark the Sabbath; mourn the dead; drive away plague; and beautify festivals.

One common feature of late mediaeval church life that was reflected in Darsham was that there was a parish gild. The gild in Darsham was known as the Gild of St Margaret. It is not known when it came into existence, but its function and property was recorded in 1548, before it was dissolved:

'One rood of meadow in Dersham. Given by whome or to what intente or purpose we knowe nott but the profitte thereof hath beene alweyes employed abowte a lampe lighte in the parysshe

This is believed to be the early
Norman font from Darsham Church
which was replaced c.1411 by the
present font given by
Geoffrey Symond, Rector of Bradwell.

It is now preserved within
the ruins of Sibton Abbey

The Garard brass
& below
The Reve brass

These two brasses
date from the years
1460 - 1500

churche o Dersham. Worth yerely iiijd whereof in rentes resolutes - null; and so remayneth clere iiijd.'

The gild owned about a rood of meadowland, the income from which was fourpence per year, and this money was used to maintain a light for devotional purposes in the parish church. Many parish gilds simply had the object of supporting such a light to burn either perpetually or on special days before the image of the saint in whose name they were enrolled. The tiny income of the gild in Darsham means that the light was only used on special days associated with St Margaret. It may have been an image of her person that stood in the niche on the south window sill.

It is uncertain when the church reached its final form, just as it is unknown when the building came to bear the dedication to All Saints. The earliest traceable reference to Darsham All Saints is in a will of John Reve, dated 1441. The church building is a mixture of work covering hundreds of years, and there are many descriptions of its architecture, but these details are outside the remit of this present work.

Chapter Two

The Reformation

Vast changes swept through Europe beginning in the early sixteenth century. These resulted from a revival of learning, and eventually they penetrated East Anglia. The Reformation is presented by many history books as a series of abrupt dislocations in England, but it was probably experienced more as phased change in Darsham. Even though the main road went through the village, one wonders how far people from Darsham travelled, perhaps the farthest that many of them ventured would have been to the markets at Saxmundham or Blythburgh, and so new ideas would arrive slowly. This was an age when people were tied to their villages. Strangers could be beggars, runagates, or worse, and their word would not be taken too seriously.

Whatever other news arrived in Darsham from the outside world, perhaps the first thing that had a direct impact was the Injunctions of 1538. These were instructions issued with the authority of the king by Thomas Cromwell. Firstly, parishes were told to provide a complete copy of the Bible in English, and to have it kept in the parish church where people could read it. The new Bible had to be in place by All Saints' Day. Clergy were told to exhort people to read the Bible, to teach their parishioners the Lord's Prayer and the Creed in English, and to explain what they meant. When that had been done, then they had to repeat the process with the Ten

The Reformation

Commandments. Clergy were also told that there had to be a sermon in each church once a quarter. It was ordered that registers of Baptism, Marriages and Burials be kept in each parish and we are fortunate that the Darsham registers from that date have survived. These were major developments in a society regulated by long term custom, but such changes were not disruptive. The only question at issue was the capacity of priests to be able to meet the requirements of the Crown as well as their own monastery. John Spenser was appointed vicar in 1532. The fact that he remained in office until 1555 speaks of local continuity.

In some places the Dissolution of the Monasteries was linked to hardship and bad practice, but elsewhere monks were placed as clergy in parishes, or else they were given pensions. Some of the abbots and priors ended their days as bishops or deans. The priory at Thetford was dissolved in 1540. The last prior was William Burden. He had been a monk at Thetford since at least 1504, was sub-prior by 1513 and elected prior by June 1518. He died in November 1540 about eight months after his priory was handed over to the Crown. At least he died peaceably, and did not suffer being hung outside the main gate of his monastery, as happened in at least three places where abbots did not co-operate with the royal agents.

Realistically, the Dissolution of the Monasteries was not a large problem as there were less than 10,000 persons under monastic vows in a population of more than three million.

The Reformation

Some monastic lands were appropriated by the Crown and sold. But there is also evidence that the families that had created ecclesiastical endowments retained a beneficent interest and even an element of control over the gifts of their ancestors and, to some extent, these monastic lands reverted to the families who had given them in the first place. Accordingly, the manor of Darsham-cum-Yoxford, along with the rights linked to Darsham parish church, passed back to the family of the Dukes of Norfolk.

One of the most far-reaching effects of the Dissolution was the passage into private hands of the right to present clergy to serve as the vicar of a parish. There were now openings for clergy from a wide variety of backgrounds.

Some things did not change, and are unchanged to this day. Law dating back before the Norman Conquest to the reigns of Ethelred the Unready and Canute has left three principles which have guided the Church in this land ever since. Firstly, once a priest has been put in possession of a church, only the bishop can deprive him of that church, and then only after the priest has been convicted of an offence for which that would be an appropriate punishment; secondly, a parish priest is under the authority of the bishop; and, thirdly, the parishioners have to take their share in the upkeep of the fabric of the church. Basically, this has meant in Darsham that there has been a continuity of service from vicars, who have not been subject to movement through administrative or episcopal caprice, and also that the people of Darsham have

The Reformation

been able to regard the church building as their church, because they have a direct interest in the fabric. A system of checks and balances evolved to make sure that priests did their duty, that the belongings of the church were accounted for by the churchwardens, and that the people did their duty, both in worship and in the care of the fabric. These duties are still investigated every year in the Visitation, carried out by the archdeacon or the rural dean, thus ensuring the health of the life of the Church.

The structure of authority that emerged with the new Tudor Age meant local people had more involvement in parish affairs. The ancient system of manorial courts had long been in decline, and the work of these courts was gradually passing to justices of the peace under the king's prerogative. At some stage, vestry meetings came into being to cope with the issues that remained a local responsibility. They were called vestry meetings simply because they were held in the church vestry. At these meetings churchwardens and the parish clerk were elected. The churchwardens were elected for a year, and the parish clerk for life, or until resignation. The churchwarden's office was probably already 250 years old and the parish clerk was an even more ancient office possibly dating back to the year 600. Other officials were also appointed who in years to come would be called the parish constable, the surveyor of the highway, and the overseer of the poor. It was not until 1894 that the civil parish became distinct from the ecclesiastical parish.

The Reformation

King Henry VIII may have been innovative in the matter of severing his kingdom from the authority of Rome, but he remained conservative in religious doctrine. His right-hand man Thomas Cromwell overstepped his master's trust. Thomas Cromwell had borne the responsibility for the Dissolution of the Monasteries and the introduction of the English Bible, but he was executed in 1540, having been condemned for treason and was not even allowed to speak in his own defence. These were dangerous times. There is no evidence that Darsham was in any way troubled by all these goings-on. In fact, people probably felt that they were living at a safe distance. They shook their heads at the tales of travellers, and knew better than to comment.

The new king, Edward VI, came to the throne in 1547. A royal Injunction in July required the books of the New Testament to be read in English at services. An Act of Parliament required that people receive both bread and wine at the Holy Communion, and then in March, 1548 English prayers were issued to be inserted within the Latin Mass. The following January, the Latin Mass was abolished, and a new English Prayer Book was directed to be used. At last those who had taken their share in the care of the building could begin to take their proper share in the worship that was offered. The prayer book was revised very soon in 1552. These prayer books were designed to teach prayers by rote and to help people to understand the prayers that were addressed to God.

The Reformation

Perhaps the congregation, and John Spencer its vicar, was still getting used to the new service book when Mary Tudor came to the throne in 1553. The Latin Mass was put back into use. However, the clock could not be turned back; the monasteries could not be re-established unless they were given new endowments because laity continued in possession of former church lands.

A new vicar, John Torre, took office in 1555. During this time the village would have listened in astonishment, turning to horror and revulsion, at news from travellers of burnings - the public burning of living people for their beliefs - condemned to death by traditionalist Roman clergy associated with Queen Mary. Included amongst the victims was the author of the English Prayer Book, Thomas Cranmer. It could all have seemed a long way away, except that thirty-six were executed by burning in Suffolk alone. There is a record that one Robert Coo, a shereman of Melford, was burnt in Yoxford Street in September, 1555. The policy of popular intimidation that made such a dreadful spectacle in Yoxford can only have backfired and convinced people in the locality in favour of the Reformation. In Darsham people have never taken kindly to being told what to think or how to think it!

It must have come as something of a relief from this turmoil when Queen Mary died in 1558 and her sister Elizabeth ascended to the throne. The church bell would have been rung for the accession of Elizabeth as it had been for the

The Reformation

accession of Mary. Vicar Torre continued in office whilst the new reign brought back the prayer book in English. Legislation required that all persons inhabiting the realm should attend their parish church, or face a fine of one shilling for each absence. Roman Catholics who refused were called recusants. The fine was raised over the years until by 1605 recusants were liable to forfeit their goods and two thirds of their real estate.

The official Recusant Rolls contain the lists of their names. Roman Catholics as well as Puritan dissenters suffered fines and forfeitures and the confiscation of property. In the 1607 Roll some recusants were recorded as applying to the Exchequer Court to be released from their sentence - on the grounds that they now conformed to the Church of England - including William Haddenham of Darsham, a yeoman. William was buried in Darsham on 23rd February, 1631.

The congregation and its vicars at Darsham enjoyed a measure of stability until well into the seventeenth century. Eventually, conflict was to arise again, but this time over which ceremonies were appropriate to church services, and whether the prayer book should be used, or no book at all. Meanwhile, life continued in the parish and rites of passage were recorded in the parish registers. Though there is no known direct descent, modern family names are there in the pages of the early register - names such as Bloomfield, Chapman, Feveryer, Reeve, Sharpe and White - and they give us a sense of continuity with those times. These early

TERRIER of Glebe Lands in Darsham
Dated 19th MARCH 1613

Nicholas Widly Clk.

One piece of Glebeland containing two acres upon it one Vicarage house.
One piece of Glebeland lying towards Brussels Green one acre more or less.
One piece of Glebeland lying......? half an acre more or less.
One piece of Glebeland lying within the lands of John Nollah some time John Reve of Buckles by estimation one roode more or less
One other piece of Glebeland lying within the land of Thomas Bedingfield Esquire called ye Pound Meadow and contained by estimation one acre more or less.

ITEM The Tithe following is payable on the kinde lambs/wool/pigs/geese/chickens/and other fowles/haye/hempe/hopes/woode/hony/waxe/...? and such like

IT For ye cowe and ye calfe threpence
IT For the gast cowe twopence
IT For a heffer two yeres not having calfe twopence
IT For a hide paying one penny; For the falle of a coult one penny
IT For a ...? yeringe coult unwrought four pence: & for every fatted beast two pence
IT A pention of fourty shillings a year yearly unto the Rectorie of Darsham to the Vicker for ye time being.
IT For a mortnavie according to the statute/ and for the burrying of the dead corps fivepence
IT For the churchinge of a wyfe sixpence/ and for the offerings of servie commitant at easter twopence.
IT For customs egges(?) upon good friday/ and for marriage of a man and his wyfe sixpence.
IT All outletted .....ing lands within the said towne doe pay yearly exchange for the same lands.

Wits: John Reve; James Hlldone?; John Toklowe; Renold Barkler; Barnard Barkler;
Robert Reve of Chenis; Henry Denny

Transcript of a 17th Century Terrier of Church property: SRO Ref: FAA: 2701/19/104

Parish Survey of 1650

DARSHAM

Darsham's Ecless(iastic) lyving is a parsonage impropriated. And a viccaridge presentative w(i)th care of soules. Phillip Bedingfeild Esq. is the improprietor and posesor of the Tithe corne and it is worth thirtye pounds pr ann(u)m. As the said improprietor is patron to the viccaridge and Mr Edmond Barker is the incumbent and viccar and receiveth the viccaridge proffitts w(hi)ch are worth about Foure and thirty poundes yearly (viz) the glebe Eight pounds the small tithes, herbage and customes Four and twentye pounds and fortye shillings payed yearly by the improprietor to the viccar as a stipend. And the church of Darsham is sittuate about a myle from Yoxford, Ubbeston, Middleton and Fordley and Thorington. And the cure is now neglected by the Incumbents absence who is removed Thirteen Myles Distant.

A transcript from the Commonwealth Records. Lambeth Palace Library.

Ref: COMM. XIIa. 15/544-6

registers were of plain parchment pages and conducive to extra notes being added at the whim of either the vicar or his parish clerk. Notes about parishioners, of collections taken for disasters or national causes, of population totals and other events were sometimes recorded. For example, we read that on 4th March, 1638, a licence was granted by the Rev. Eachard, the Vicar, to Mr Thomas Southwell to eat meat in Lent, he being aged 82 and sickly. He paid 6s.8d for this dispensation for the use of the poor in Darsham.

Chapter Three

Later Tudors and Early Stuarts

The English Prayer Book was revised in 1559. It would be a mistake to think that the Elizabethan Settlement led the parish churches of England into any routine and rhythm of the services of the English Prayer Book familiar to us. How were the church services conducted, and how did people participate? Most of the congregation would not have been able to follow the service: they would not have been able to read, and there would have been very few books for them to use.

Services in parish churches would not have been much like they are today, even though the familiar words of our traditional prayer books are still almost the same. None-the-less a pattern emerged with the prayer book becoming part of the life of the church. The same prayer book being used throughout the country, participation in the worship of the Church became a token of patriotism and national identity.

In 1562, there was a contribution to public worship almost equal in importance to the prayer book. This was the publication of the psalms in verse form, with tunes to which they could be sung. It is sometimes referred to as 'Daye's Psalter'. John Daye was a publisher in London and he would have known Darsham, because he was a native of Dunwich.

The official title of the book was:

> '𝕱𝖍𝖊 𝖂𝖍𝖔𝖑𝖊 𝕭𝖔𝖔𝖐𝖊 𝖔𝖋 𝕻𝖘𝖆𝖑𝖒𝖊𝖘 𝕮𝖔𝖑𝖑𝖊𝖈𝖙𝖊𝖉 into 𝕰𝖓𝖌𝖑𝖎𝖘𝖍 𝕸𝖊𝖊𝖙𝖊𝖗 by 𝕿𝖍𝖔𝖒𝖆𝖘 𝕾𝖙𝖊𝖗𝖓𝖍𝖔𝖑𝖉, 𝕵𝖔𝖍𝖓 𝕳𝖔𝖕𝖐𝖎𝖓𝖘, and others: conferred with the 𝕳𝖊𝖇𝖗𝖊𝖜, with apt notes to sing them withall. Set forth and allowed to be sung in all Churches, of all the people together, before and after Morning and Evening Prayer, as also before & after Sermons: and moreover in private houses, for their godly solace and comfort, laying apart all ungodly songs and Ballads, which tend only to the nourishing of vice, and corrupting of youth'.

The title seems peculiarly long to us - but it functioned as both advertisement and licence. Over the next two centuries hundreds of thousands of copies were printed. The text was often printed at the back of copies of the Book of Common Prayer, and this metrical version of the psalms came to ensure popular participation in church services. The translation of Psalm 100 still features in our hymn books - 'All people that on earth do dwell, sing to the Lord with cheerful voice...', and is still sung to the same tune after 450 years. When such material is used how closely we are treading in the steps of our predecessors in this village, and is not the present moment a very thin veneer barely covering the past?

The metrical psalms came to be incorporated in the layout of the typical Sunday morning service that evolved in the Parish Church on this pattern: metrical psalm, Morning Prayer, metrical psalm, Litany, Ante-Communion, metrical psalm, sermon, and finally another metrical psalm. The Lord's Supper, the Holy Communion, came to be very infrequent in many churches, four times a year becoming a maximum.

The metrical psalms were chosen by the parish clerk. It was a mercy that *whole* metrical psalms were not necessarily sung at each stage of the proceedings because of the sheer length of time that it took to render these psalms. To allow for the fact that many could not read or did not have copies, the parish clerk would announce the psalm, and then read each line that was to be sung before the congregation rendered it in song. There were only a few tunes, but each congregation would ornament these tunes in their own way which would have made the tunes sung at Darsham very different from the same tunes sung at Westleton or Yoxford. These psalms were normally sung with full voice and extremely slowly, at a speed of only about one minute per line. The results were a remarkable emotional and spiritual experience of full-throated shared participation, totally unlike anything that we may associate with the modern versions of Anglican tradition.

Later Tudors & Early Stuarts

The differing local usages of the prayer book and metrical psalter (especially given inevitable clerical eccentricity) meant that worship became a symbol of unique parish identity. The offering of worship in the parish church, as well as affirming a national identity, became closely linked to a locality and the community within it.

The congregation was encouraged to join in the whole service, but it was in this era that people began to use the phrase to 'hear the service'. In between the metrical psalm singing the service was conducted by the minister, and the people's part was taken by their elected representative - the parish clerk. The appointed psalms and the canticles of morning and evening prayer were read with vicar and the clerk taking alternate verses. The congregation were encouraged to join in - but many writers commented upon the lack of general participation in services during the next century and a half. More is written in a later chapter about the last of the parish clerks of Darsham, Mr Billy Bezant (who died in 1901), but it is worth noting here that he maintained the traditional role of his office so that his strong voice was to be heard leading the singing and responses at services.

Some may smile at the length of the church services at this time in our history. When there was a sermon, a service could have lasted two and a half hours. When a sermon was not offered by the parson, there was an official book of sermons called 'The Book of Homilies' from which the parson could read, and then worship could have taken even longer. However the subtle aspects to Anglican worship at this time ranging from the creation and affirmation of a national identity to the consolidation and healing of local communities, meant that the length of the Anglican service gave time for worship and a time for all these other elements to find expression.

Chapter Four

Civil War and Restoration

The Civil War and the Interregnum following the execution of Charles I in 1649 were times of disorganisation and chaos. The ideals that drove the revolution were partly religious - and sought to purify the life of the Church in England.

During the period of the Commonwealth (1649-60), marriages in church were not allowed but were to be performed in a civil ceremony by a magistrate, so we have no record of these. There were only three burials recorded during these years. The administrative system of parish registers had collapsed. The vicar for the first part of these years of dislocation was John Eachard. His father was Christopher Echard of Gt. Yarmouth and his mother Anne (née Lawrence) came from Fressingfield. He married Judith Coate of Upton, Norfolk, and baptised his six children in Darsham between 1623 and 1636. He died and was buried in Darsham in 1647 and his will of 1644 mentions his lands in Darsham & Upton, fish houses in Yarmouth, and his house in Dunwich. He had at least three of his sermons published and copies are preserved in the Bodleian Library, Oxford. Eachard had been presented to be vicar by the Bedingfield family, acting as patrons. The Bedingfields, as the holders of Darsham Hall, had tremendous local influence. The largest of the three brasses in the aisle of the church commemorates Anne Bedingfield who died in 1641, she was the wife of

Civil War and Restoration

Eustace Bedingfield of Holme Hale in Norfolk and related to the Darsham Hall family. A large wall monument to Sir Thomas Bedingfield of Darsham Hall commemorates his death. He held several titles, not least as one of the judges at the Court of Common Pleas during the reign of King Charles I.

This Thomas Bedingfield was born about 1593. As a lawyer, he rose to become the Recorder of London. But as the tension between Crown and Parliament developed, his career became overshadowed by the dangers of the times. In 1642 the King attempted to arrest five Members of Parliament whilst the House of Commons was sitting. This self-defeating attempt to assert royal authority led to all sorts of recriminations. Before long, the Attorney-General was impeached by the Commons for his share in the King's plans, and the House of Lords directed Thomas Bedingfield to act as a defence counsel. When he dithered about his role he was sent to the Tower to allow him time to reflect.

Was he more decisive in his allegiance in the early stages of the Civil War - or was he more favourably disposed to the parliamentary side? We do not know, but quite definitely the execution of the King in 1649 made him draw the line under his involvements in London, and he retired to his family home at Darsham Hall. The tablet on the north wall of the chancel records that he was:

17th Century Brass of
Anne Bedingfield
who died in 1641

Anno 1649

Relict Brown was buried the 29th of May Anno suprascript

Robert Newton was buried the 17th of September Anno sixty[...]

William Bale the sone of Thomas Bale was [...] buried the fifteenth day of October anno [...] suprascript.

John Bale the sone of Thomas Bale was buried the [...] day of October Anno [...]

Anne Huddinham the daughter of william Huddinham was buried the 4th of march

Robert the sone of william Huddinham was buried the 13 of march Anno 1650

[...] the [...] of Richard Brown was buried the 17th of [...]

Mary the daughter of Alexandre Burrant was buried the 18th day of Aug. 1650

Mary the daughter of William Betts was buried the 14th of September 1651

Thomas Bedingfeild knight was buried the ——— 1661:
27th of Martij

Mr Anthony Bedinfeild the son of Squire Bedinfeild was buried 662 the 17 day of December 1662

Susanna Bidinfield the Daughter of Nicholas Bidinfield was buried the 4th of february anno predicto.

1666 John Short was buried the 20 of December

**A page from Darsham Burial Register
showing the 1661 entry for the
burial of Sir Thomas Bedingfield.**

**Signatures of Darsham Men
who took the
Oath of Protestation in 1641**

THE OATH OF PROTESTATION - 1641

Charles I

In 1641, Parliament organised a protest against the possibility of "an arbitrary and tyrannical government". The oath to uphold the True Protestant Religion was read out in every parish church and was to be signed by every male over the age of 18 years. Those who refused to sign were deemed unfit to hold public office.

In Darsham, the oath was read out by the Rev. John Echard and the following list of the Darsham men who signed, between the 7th November 1641 and 25th February 1641, appears in the back of the first Darsham Parish Register for 1536-1744.

(S.R.O.Ref: FC 65/D1/1)

Thomas Cobbold	Robart Hayward	
Valentine Perce	John Byshe	William Harte
William Hadnam	John Bedingfield	Henry Jordan
Richard Staffe	Robart Reeve	Robert Scoulding
John Reeve	Robert Poley	Richard Wade
John Short	Edward Artis	Robert Browne
John Beart	Edward Poley	Simon Stannard
Walter Pilborrou	Richard Bottrit	Nicholas Brown
William Mosse	William Wentford	John Ellis
George Steele	William Scut	Peter Martin
John Petch	Nicholas Beningfield	Edm.Backler
Thomas Steele	Thomas Poley	Gregory White
Daniel Alen	John Baldery	Richard Mollett
Simon Crispe	Phillip Primrose	Wm Mickleborough
William Reeve	Alexander Durrant	John Newson
Samuel Mouser	George Mouser	Robert Mils
Richard Dut	William Tollifer	Richard Andrews
Ezekiel Ellis	Owen Backler	Henry Foster
Robert Mowser	Arthur Ellis	Richard Church
Samuell ?	John Hammond	William Edwards

Civil War and Restoration

'made Attorney Generall of ye Dutchy of Lancaster and one of the Judges of the Court of Common Pleas by King Charles the 1st of blessed memory. Upon whose murder, he layd downe his place & all publiq imployments, retiring himselfe to this Towne, where he dyed March the 24th 1660 being about 68 yeares of Age'.

Thomas Bedingfield lived to see the restoration of King Charles II, and the reassertion of the constitution. In those days, the number of the year was changed on Lady Day, the feast of the Annunciation, being nine months before Christmas Day. So by our reckoning he died in 1661.

The upheaval of those times was not only marked in Darsham by Sir Thomas Bedingfield's withdrawal to the safety of the countryside. In 1641, Parliament organised a protest against the possibility of 'an arbitrary and tyrannical government'. This was known as The Oath of Protestation. It had to be signed by every male over the age of 18 years. Those who refused to sign were deemed unfit to hold public office.

In Darsham, the oath was read out by Vicar Eachard and the list of the Darsham men who signed, between the 7th November 1641 and 25th February 1642, appears in the back of the first Darsham parish register. The list of 59 signatures

Civil War and Restoration

or 'marks' of Darsham men is an unusual piece of historical evidence. Darsham is one of the few Suffolk parishes for which this list has survived.

In 1645 Parliament decreed the abolition of the Book of Common Prayer and issued a 'Directory of Public Worship' to be used instead. This book gave an outline for the contents of the services of the Church, rather than specifying exactly what was to be done at every stage. In practice, some congregations ignored it and continued to use the old book, some welcomed the new freedom and would experiment enthusiastically, and some clergy were known to memorise the services of the old prayer book so that they could conform to the new 'directory' whilst also maintaining the old familiar phrases. Vicar Eachard had to please all sides in this contention, but then he was succeeded by Samuel Golby in about 1647. By this time new appointments were scrutinised by committees set up for this purpose and it may fairly safely be assumed that Samuel Golby would have been a man to use the freedoms of the new directory, even if he subsequently offended local opinion by living away from the parish and employing a curate.

It was in the spirit of the times that Parliament did more than issue a new service book, abolish episcopal ministry, and interfere in the workings of the parish. Parliament came to see itself as a divine agent for the work of completing the Reformation. They felt that the changes begun under Henry VIII had not gone far enough. As part of their programme,

Civil War and Restoration

Parliament decided that it was essential to suppress religious art and church decoration. There was a particular frenzy to do this work in the Eastern counties, and Parliament appointed an officer to regulate church ornament in the county of Suffolk. His name was William Dowsing and, strangely, he kept some notes of his pilgrimage of vandalism as he, and the men under his direction, smashed sculptures, stained glass, paintings and inscriptions. His 'Journal' records that on April 9th, 1643, Dowsing went from Dunwich to Bramfield. He would almost certainly have passed through Westleton and Darsham, and if he did not come himself, then his immediate companions would have checked the churches.

He normally only recorded particular places in his Journal if there were 'superstitious pictures' to be demolished. He certainly wrote that he ordered the demolition of the chancel cross on All Saints', Dunwich. And it is quite likely that he was involved in the destruction of the gable-end cross on St. Peter's Westleton. Dowsing may well have instigated some damage to the tower parapet at Darsham. Many mediaeval church towers carried large crosses on the top, set in the parapet. The day before (April 8th), Dowsing had ordered the destruction of two crosses on the tower at Frostenden. Until 1991, Darsham church tower had long-standing damage on the north and south sides of the parapet in the centre, which had been poorly repaired, and it is quite likely that two crosses had been torn off. In the vestry, at the bottom of the tower, there are fragments of ancient stained glass incorporated into the window. These small pieces of glass may well come from a window that was smashed at this time.

Civil War and Restoration

Be that as it may, creative work was being done soon inside the tower to install a new bell frame. Three bells were cast in 1656 and hung in the tower. By this time custom dictated an extra function for village bells: they were expected to be rung if someone important went through the village. With the main road going past the church, it was rather a disgrace to have only one bell to toll. Evidence has survived from elsewhere in the country of dignitaries levying fines upon a village if the bells were not rung to acknowledge their progress. These three bells sound well in their tonal relationship to each other, but sound curious when rung with the older bell. By 1976, the ancient bells and their bell-frame were deteriorating and pull ropes were installed to enable the bells to be chimed. This ended the problem of the shortage of bell-ringers which had meant that the three smaller bells would often have to rung by one person using two hands and one foot!

As the Interregnum wore on, traditional Anglican patterns of devotion came to seem more attractive. People became tired of endless experiment and innovation, and after all the uncertainties of these years they yearned for stability. The Restoration of Charles II in 1660 promptly brought the Book of Common Prayer back into use. Again in Darsham there was some continuity through these changing times. Samuel Golby continued as vicar until 1683. Darsham proved to be a compassionate place under his ministry. This is an opportunity to mention some more of the notes inscribed in the parish registers. In 1661 a collection amounting to 6s.9d

Civil War and Restoration

was taken for the Protestants of Lithuania; in 1671 a collection amounting to £9.13s.0d was taken towards the redemption of Turkish slaves; and in 1674 a collection amounting to £10.7s.9d was taken for the relief of the poor of Halesworth when that town was visited by the smallpox. For such a small community to be so outward looking was remarkable.

In 1683, a new vicar was appointed called Thomas Warren. He had evidently commended himself to the Bedingfield family as the patrons of the living, as it is noted that he had been acting as assistant curate in the parish. It was not long, however, before Vicar Warren had to cope with a tragedy that affected the future of the Bedingfields in Darsham and the whole future life of the village.

In 1684, Thomas Bedingfield, the heir to the estates of Darsham Hall, was murdered at Norwich. Documents from the time relate that this murder took place while the Assizes were being held at Norwich. Early in the morning of Sunday 20th July, 1684, an argument arose between two contemporaries who had been drinking, and Thomas Bedingfield was murdered. The accused, Thomas Barney, had a week in prison before being brought before a court. The jury had no hesitation in pronouncing his guilt, and he was duly hanged at Norwich Market Cross. This murder was regarded as peculiarly shocking because it happened whilst the Assizes were sitting, and that was reckoned to be a direct affront to royal authority. Also, as it happened on a Sunday,

Civil War and Restoration

it was felt to be an act of direct contempt towards the Church. Remarkably, a contemporary sermon has survived in the Norwich Record Office, the title of which reflects the level of disgust felt at this event:

> 'Joab's bloody Complement to Abner set forth in a sermon occasioned by the much lamented death & cruell murther of Thomas Beddingfield of Darsham Hall Esq. by Thomas Berney gent. in the Citty of Norwich, July 20 1684 preached at Carlton Colville in Suffolk by John Browne Minister there.'

The following words are taken from an 'Elegy on the Death of Thomas Beddingfield' that was published in London:

> 'The Hearts of Men can never be at Ease,
> Till they with floods of Grief their Souls appease:
> For he who doth not this lov'd Man Bemoan,
> His Heart's composed of Adamantine-Stone:
> Yet all the Tears are offerr'd by your Eyes,
> And all the Griefs relenting Hearts comprize,
> Are due to him, as his just Obsequies.
> The Countrys Darling, and Mankinds Delight,
> Is snatch'd as on a sudden from our Sight.
> But Reader think he was prepar'd to Dye,

Civil War and Restoration

Whose Life was Vertue and Morality.
Envy it self, could ne're eclips his Fame,
His Life was Innocent and void of Blame:
His business on the Earth was doing Good,
And 'twas as customary as his Food.
He was all Mildness and good Nature, he
Was Exercis'd in works of Charity:
The Scale of all his Actions were so even,
He was too good for Earth, and's gone to Heaven.'

The Darsham estates passed to the Rous family of Henham through Thomas Bedingfield's sister Philippa who had married Sir John Rous, 2nd bart, in 1676. Something of the community died with him as the village became a branch of the Henham estates.

Chapter Five

The Eighteenth Century

England and Scotland were united in 1707, and the House of Hanover succeeded to the throne in 1714, but these affairs of state would make little difference locally. The century was to be marked by England's repeated participation in major wars, and it would be surprising if some of the young men of Darsham did not venture abroad in the service of the king. If ever they came back home, they probably found Darsham much as it had been when they went away. The soil was still as difficult to work, but work was the only thing that kept poverty at bay.

During the early part of the eighteenth century there was widespread distress in Suffolk owing to the spread of unemployment. This was to be a long and drawn-out problem and, like so many social problems, people tended to avoid dealing with it for as long as possible. Laws dating from the reign of Queen Elizabeth had established that each parish should look after its own, and only its own. Everybody had to have a parish in which he or she was deemed to be 'settled' - usually, the parish of birth. It was expected that work should be made available to those who needed it and parish workhouses were to be provided for this purpose, but parish workhouses could rarely cover the costs of providing work. Whatever the inmates did could usually be done cheaper by established tradesmen. An Act of 1723 enabled groups of parishes to combine for the purpose of building and

The Eighteenth Century

running a workhouse. In 1764 this system of poor relief was inaugurated in our district. All the parishes within the Hundred of Blything (except Dunwich where there seemed to be internal disagreements) were incorporated for the maintenance of the poor in a 'House of Industry' at Bulcamp.

The first meeting of the directors and guardians of the proposed Blything Union Workhouse was held at the Angel Hotel, Halesworth, in 1764, and consisted of local dignitaries, farmers, and clergy. Those from Darsham were Sir John Rous of Darsham Hall, Charles Purvis of Darsham House, and the Revd. Robert Buxton, vicar of Darsham. The first bricks were laid on 18th March 1765, when several of the directors including Vicar Buxton were present, each laying a brick in turn. The workhouse was not opened until 1766 when fifty six paupers were admitted. The cause of the delay was that the construction of the 'House' caused so much discontent that the partly built house was wrecked in a riot in August, 1765. People from various villages joined the mob that attacked the building site. On 10th August, 1765, the *Ipswich Journal* printed a letter from a correspondent in Halesworth:

'You may depend upon the truth of the following account of what happened in our neighbourhood last Monday about five o'clock in the evening. The rioters to the number of about two hundred, went through this town to Bulcamp, where the workhouse was building, about five miles hence. A few of them mounted the works and climbed to the top of the poles

The Eighteenth Century

of the scaffold, waved their hats and huzza'd: in about half an hour there was a much greater number of people and by nine o'clock at night, the whole building was levelled to the ground. The joists of the chamber floor were laid bare, and the damage is computed at £2,000. After doing this mischief they went to Sir John Rous's house at Henham where, upon their demand of refreshment, they had plenty of beer and victuals given them; from hence they went to George Golding's Esq, at Thorington, who was not at home, but they called up the steward, who was obliged to give them what provision the house afforded. They went off very quietly from thence to the Revd. Mr Buxton's at Darsham, so through Yoxford to Sir John Scrivener's Esq, at Sibton, and demanded further refreshment, and then returned to Yoxford, and desired to speak with Mr Ingham of that place, who was not at home: They began to pull down his house, but were prevailed on by some people present to desist. What these people will attempt further, time will discover.'

What are the factors responsible for such behaviour? Concerned people were beginning to investigate what happened to those who were put in the workhouse. One writer described them as 'mansions of putridity'. Pauper children often did not survive. The workhouses were seen as a terrible fate rather than a solution to a problem, and some figures quoted later on in this chapter bear this out. There were a lot of rumours around at the time of inmates being in the workhouse for life, of them being whipped, incarcerated in dungeons and some being transported. The authorities

BLYTHING CORPORATION WORKHOUSE
BULCAMP HOUSE OF INDUSTRY

Conditions of life in the House were laid down at the meeting on the 10th March, 1766. Stocks of clothing and shoes for the inmates were paid for in the July, and at the meeting on 22nd September, 1766, details of the menu were settled:

	Breakfast	Dinner	Supper
Sun	Bread & Cheese or Butter	Boiled Beef, Dumplings & Roots	Bread & Cheese or Butter
Mon	Bread & Cheese or Butter	Peas Pottage with Beef Broth & Dumplings	Milk Broth
Tue	Milk Broth	Boiled Beef, Dumplings & Roots	Bread & Cheese or Butter
Wed	Bread & Cheese or Butter	Peas Pottage with Beef Broth & Dumplings	Bread & Cheese or Butter
Thu	Milk Broth or Butter	Baked Suet Puddings	Bread & Cheese
Fri	Bread & Cheese or Butter	Boiled Pork & Peas & Dumplings	Peas Pottage
Sat	Milk Broth	Rice Milk or Frumenty	Bread & Cheese or Butter

The Commissioners' Report of 1836 compared the diets of the Houses of Industry in Norfolk & Suffolk. Bulcamp Workhouse appears to have been average for the list with weekly total of food as follows:

Solid food — i.e. Bread, Cheese, Cooked meat, Dumplings etc: ... 210 ozs
Meat or Milk Broth, Soup, Rice Milk etc .... 4½ pts
Vegetables .... 16 ozs
Beer .... 7 pts

Compared to the Soldiers of the Line at that time, whose rations were 168 oz of solid food per week, and the estimated average diet of the independent agricultural labourer, which did not exceed 122 ozs, the inmates of the workhouse were not considered underfed by comparison.

continued:

The House was opened in October, 1766 and after an initial 56 paupers on the first day, by April 1767 there were 356 in residence. At this stage families were not separated although the single inmates were segregated. It appears that the inmates were allowed to bring in their own beds and bedding, providing that it was clean, together with some of their own personal possessions.

On admission, they were provided with workhouse clothing, their own being washed and stored ready for return on discharge.
The men wore "half-thick Yorkshire" claret cloaks, leather breeches and caps; the women had brown "Padua" serge cloaks, grey Lindsey gowns with baize undergowns, and bonnets with strings. Shirts and shifts were of Suffolk hempen cloth.

Inmates were discharged to find work, particularly at harvest time and were allowed discharge at their own request if they were able to support themselves.

The Corporation was dissolved in July 1835 by the Directors and acting Guardians and a new Union was formed under the control of the New Poor Law Commissioners. The workhouse was altered in 1836.

It was later to become the Blythburgh Hospital for the sick, finally to be closed in 1994.

Refs: *Suffolk R.O. — ADA/AB3/1 Minute Book 1764 - 1766*
"The Poor Law in Norfolk" 1700 - 1850

---

from the *HALESWORTH TIMES*, Tuesday, 28th June 1887

QUEEN's JUBILEE

Bulcamp: The Guardians of the Blything Union provided a capital dinner for their humble wards, the inmates of the Union House, on Jubilee Day. The dinner of Plum Pudding and Roast Beef was well cooked, and served by the Master and Matron, Mr & Mrs Caton, assisted by other officers. Some capital mottoes were displayed over the entrance gates, which were further supplemented by a goodly supply of flags and bunting.

The Eighteenth Century

had to issue denials in the newspapers and to circulate printed pamphlets stating that the rumours were not true and that inmates would be discharged at their own request if they found work to support themselves. Punishment would only be for refusing to work, for misdemeanours and insubordination. There was clearly a great deal of fear associated with the local workhouses, and there was similar unrest connected with workhouses at Wickham Market and Nacton.

One of our churchyard headstones perhaps summarises people's feelings during these years:

> 'My Sledge & Hammer are reclin'd
> My Bellows too have lost their Wind
> My Fire extinct my Forge decay'd
> And in the dust my Vice is laid
> My Coals are spent my Iron gone
> My Nails are drove my work is done'

This was a memorial to Jeremiah Eastaugh, a blacksmith, who died in March 1788, aged 69 years. He lived in the dwelling now known as Garden Cottage. The poem appears in other parts of the country, its origin unknown. The difficulties of a time when the work and skills of so many were overtaken by the technological progress of the agricultural revolution cannot be overestimated. However, without such changes poverty and starvation could only have increased in the long term. It was becoming possible to

The Eighteenth Century

cultivate light soils that were cheaper to farm, and our local heavy soils could not compete.

Progress did not always work against the individual. In 1763 James Upson was the first person in the village to submit to inoculation against smallpox by Robert Sutton, the doctor who was responsible for introducing this practice. Some three months later Dame Lydia Rous at Darsham Hall, together with six of her servants, were inoculated.

Other changes were affecting local economics. In 1684, something of the soul of the ancient village had died with Thomas Bedingfield. Now a different kind of event seemed to stop the heartbeat of the village altogether. From 1785 traffic no longer used the main road through Darsham - the turnpike had been opened from Yoxford to Blythburgh, and this development confirmed the isolation and the poverty of the village.

This work is a history of the Church in Darsham, and it could be asked what the Church was doing in the midst of all this distress. During this period, many villages were so poor that a parson would sometimes hold the post of vicar in a cluster of villages, otherwise his right to collect tithes would have been oppressive. Thus, William Kett, who was vicar from 1789 to 1832, was also variously rector of Shottesham and Waldringfield from time to time. This was the age of the poverty-stricken country curate, paid a pittance by the vicar, sharing in the circumstances of the village. Sometimes the

The Eighteenth Century

curate's idealism was crushed by the surrounding misery, occasionally the curate lived outside the village altogether, returning only to take services on a Sunday. Meanwhile, the Old Version of the metrical psalms contained many references to the poor and acknowledged God's compassion for and protection of the destitute. Can we hope that our forebears found divine comfort to make their recurring distress bearable?

The church was drawn into the establishment of the Bulcamp workhouse because the vestry meeting was the decision-making organ of the village. The vicar was the chairman of the vestry meeting, and had to take a lead in trying to do something about the poverty of the time. Admittedly Vicar Buxton had married into the Rous family, and may have been more inclined towards severity to the poor rather than compassion. If he was enthusiastic about the workhouse, it may have been out of bafflement and frustration that whatever had been done to alleviate poverty, the conditions of the poor in the village were getting worse. Perhaps it was felt that at least with the building of the workhouse they were making an effort to improve the situation for some of the villagers in Darsham. The Darsham vestry meeting had to appoint an Overseer of the Poor to deal with the out-relief. He had to organise assistance for the poor who were not actually in the workhouse. The vestry meeting also had to nominate a guardian to serve on the Union Board of Guardians. Parishes were responsible for the upkeep of their own paupers in the house of industry. Each

The Eighteenth Century

year the parish was expected to take at least one pauper out of the house and to allocate that person to a local employer who would receive £5 from the Parish Poor Rate.

In the first week of opening in October 1766 there were five admissions from Darsham to the workhouse: three boys - Samuel Harris, John Plant and John Coleman, all aged 7 years; Mary Coleman aged 9 years; and Elizabeth Ives a 63 year old woman. Of these, John Coleman died the following year, the other two boys were removed from the workhouse two years later. Mary Coleman was discharged after one year (she would then have been old enough to work), and Elizabeth Ives died in the workhouse in 1769.

The first complete family from Darsham to be taken into the workhouse was the Penny family. They were admitted in January, 1767 and the family consisted of Henry Penny aged 42, his wife Elizabeth aged 33, and four children - Mary aged 11, Harvey aged 7, Susanna aged 4 and Beth aged 3 months. Of this family, the baby died in April, Mary was taken out of the house the following year by Walter Snell, a farmer of Darsham; the parents, Henry and Elizabeth were both discharged in June 1774, presumably having found work but not being able to support the remaining two children. The daughter Susanna was taken out of the house in 1776, aged 14, by James Pead of Darsham, and her brother Harvey was discharged in March, 1777, probably to a job. Henry Penny's work lasted for only two months, maybe due to illness, and he and his wife were back in the house by September, 1774.

The Eighteenth Century

Henry Penny died a month later, aged 49, in October, 1774. His wife was discharged in December, 1774. After that there is no record of the family in documents relating to Darsham. Between October, 1766 and the end of 1799 there were 133 admissions to the workhouse from Darsham, some of which were readmissions. Of these 133 admissions, 22 died, 14 ran away, and 8 boys and 8 girls were taken out of the house by employers. It is difficult to argue that such a system did much for those who were enlisted in the workhouse; all it achieved was to remove surplus people from the village economy.

The level of poverty in Darsham in this century meant that it was a place from which to get away. Of 304 people baptised in Darsham in the years 1701-1750, 238 were not buried in Darsham churchyard. This statistic implies a very high level of mobility and escape, despite the Poor Law provisions. Of 470 people baptised in the years 1751-1800, 324 were not buried in Darsham. These figures imply economic deterioration in the village because greater numbers of people left the village as the century wore on. Equally significant is the fact that 27 infants were buried in the years 1701-1750, but 63 were buried in the second half of the century; this accelerating infant mortality is another indicator of deepening poverty. This was the period of Goldsmith's *'The deserted village'* and Gray's *'Elegy written in a country churchyard'*. These figures give weight to some lines of Thomas Gray:

> 'Perhaps in this neglected spot is laid
> Some heart once pregnant with celestial fire;
> Hands, that the rod of empire might have sway'd,
> Or wak'd to extasy the living lyre.
>
> But knowledge to their eyes her ample page
> Rich with the spoils of time did ne'er unroll;
> Chill Penury repress'd their noble rage,
> and froze the genial current of the soul.'

The French Revolution was a response to living conditions even more desperate than those to be found in Darsham. The ensuing war with Napoleon perhaps rescued something of the rural life of England by encouraging social cohesion in response to a common enemy.

The Nineteenth Century

Chapter Six

The Nineteenth Century

In 1801, the nation was involved in the war with Napoleon and it was not yet half way through. In March, 1801, Admiral Nelson arrived at Yarmouth in H.M.S. St. George, having been second-in-command of the Fleet at the battle of Copenhagen. The wounded were landed at Yarmouth and were carried in wagons to London along the Yarmouth to London road and Darsham parishioners would have been well aware of their passing.

A national census was undertaken, and it was recorded that the population of Darsham in 1801 was 421. 73 families lived in 42 houses. Human fertility is a measure of health and so it seems the overall health of the village improved in the first half of the nineteenth century as 777 children were brought to baptism at the parish church - almost equal to the total for the whole of the previous century. Alas, 64 infants were buried in the first half of the century, but as a proportion of the total number of children baptised this figure shows a significant reduction in infant mortality. Maybe there was an improved diet available in the village which would have explained the apparent improvement in the situation of villagers; maybe there was more work; maybe it could have been something as simple as the introduction of commercially produced cheap soap which explains these figures.

The Nineteenth Century

The highest population ever recorded for Darsham was in 1841 when there were 528 people in 106 inhabited houses. Since then the population has gradually fallen. Notice the extraordinarily high proportion of the village who would have been children, and it is possible that a few of these left their mark in a most endearing way by scoring one of the church pews so that it could be used for 'shove-halfpenny'. Perhaps they carved their names on a village tree and their marks have been lost. But some found a most surprising way of leaving a memorial to their youth and energy. The window near the font with diamond panes of clear old glass was restored in 1985. If we look closely at the panes towards the bottom of the window, we see that there are five names scratched into the glass. They are: G or C.A. Jordan, Charles English, J. Hill, John Wink & John Brunning. The names were probably scratched on the outside, because it was easier to reach, somewhere between 1815 and 1820.

Nothing is known about the name Jordan which does not appear in either the church registers or the censuses. But Charles English was baptised in the church in October, 1800, the son of George & Elizabeth English. The name John Brunning appears in three generations of the family in the village. The first John married to Hannah Page in 1782; another John was baptised in November, 1800, the son of John & Eleanor Brunning. It was probably this John who would have been contemporary with Charles English. There is no indication which John Wink scratched his name in the glass. The earliest John Wink born about 1767, was a

The Nineteenth Century

carpenter of Brussels Green and arrived in the village about 1793, aged 26 years, and it was this family who was awarded a parcel of land, now known as Wink's Isle, when Brussels Green was enclosed in 1851. John Wink's wife Mary died in 1801 and he married for a second time a year later. Children of both marriages were baptised in Darsham and he died here in 1846. His son John Wink was born in 1792 and married in 1819 so we must assume that it was this John Wink whose name appears on the window. Perhaps the others climbed on his shoulders!

These were part of a mobile population. Of the 777 candidates baptised at the parish church in the first half of the nineteenth century, only 142 were ever buried in Darsham churchyard - less than 20%. Some families like the Jordans were transient residents in Darsham, but some residents came for longer, and became part of village life. The Flegg family had arrived in Darsham by 1861 and settled in Cheyney Green, in the area of Fox Corner, having moved there from Middleton. Mr Flegg had been born at Theberton. The Fleggs had a son called Frederick who was born in 1867, and their grandson, another Frederick, was baptised in the parish church in 1904. 'Young Mr Flegg' is seeing the millennium out in his native Darsham, having had a hard working life. A respected athlete as a young man, he has been village postman, bell ringer, and churchwarden, amongst other duties. In 1985 the Annual Parochial Church Meeting made Mr Flegg 'Churchwarden Emeritus' in order to thank him for his work in the church and the village, thus freeing him from

The Nineteenth Century

administrative tasks and allowing him to continue his unique work. The Smith family had arrived by 1871, and settled in Trustans Farm. Their clan can claim Mr Nelson Smith and Mrs Ruth Kerridge as modern descendants.

Over the years, vicars have been required to answer questions concerning parish valuations and to provide numbers of worshippers, population figures, and details of church property. The official ten-year population census had begun in 1801, and in 1851 an Ecclesiastical census was also taken in every parish. Darsham Church was alleged to have space for 184 people, 100 of which were free sittings. The average number of worshippers during the previous twelve months had been 50 for morning service and 80 for the afternoon service. Meanwhile, it was reported that Darsham Chapel had space for 182 people, 110 of which were free sittings. The chapel claimed an average congregation of 100 during the preceding 12 months, and an average attendance of 80 Sunday scholars. The population of Darsham in 1851 was 462; 260 of these were Darsham born. All the remainder were born in the surrounding area of Suffolk, except four from Norfolk, and three from London. By the time of the 1881 census, there were 628 people in the British Isles who claimed to have been born in Darsham. However, only 176 of them were still living in Darsham, 328 were living elsewhere in East Anglia, 47 were living in London and Middlesex, 60 were living in the Southern Counties, and 17 in the Midlands and the North. None had moved as far as Scotland or Wales. It would be an interesting arithmetical

The Nineteenth Century

exercise to calculate how long it will be before almost everyone in the country will probably be descended from someone born in Darsham!

The Royal Arms of George IV, as temporal head of the Church of England, and the hatchments of members of the Purvis family of Darsham House are displayed in the church. George IV was king between 1820 and 1830, and the display of the royal arms was considered to be a statement of patriotism as well as an icon of the power of the monarch. This was a short reign following the long years of George III (1760 - 1820), but there were enormous social developments. In 1824 an act was passed allowing workmen who were seeking employment to travel to different parts of the country, recognising a stark reality of rural life. In 1825 there were riots and great distress amongst the poor because of national financial instability. Did the experience of nearly disastrous social disruption provoke a desire to install the royal arms as a visible sign of order? Would the installation of Purvis hatchments have been presumptuous if the royal arms had not been present? we cannot know. The Purvis family had arrived in Darsham when Captain George Purvis, R.N., married while he was staying with the Bedingfields at Darsham Hall. He built Darsham House in 1679 to be a dwelling to give the impression of comparable social status. Later members of the family served in the navy. One was High Sheriff of Suffolk in 1794 and another was a Colonel of the Royal Dragoons. The last Purvis to be buried at Darsham was Arthur (1813-1877) who had been in the Madras Civil

The Nineteenth Century

Service. No direct evidence has survived of any significant involvement by the family in the affairs of the village. They had other houses in Bath, Brighton and London and moved among them during the seasons. Darsham House became more important for the village later on in the century. Meanwhile, the Purvis family were commemorated by wall tablets and stained glass windows.

The 19th century burial registers record some sad and notable entries: a three year old burnt to death; a two year old accidentally drowned; the burial at midnight of a smallpox victim; an 18 year old burnt to death in the early hours after the 'Harvest Home' at Priory Farm; a man killed by a cow; and a woman's suicide. Vicar Weddall had come to Darsham in 1832, probably at the age of about 25. He lived at Yoxford during his ministry because the Vicarage in Darsham was too dilapidated. In 1843 he became responsible for Dunwich Church as well. He died in 1851, aged about 44. His successor Thomas Mayhew was also the minister at Dunwich, though he lived at Westleton Grange. His ministry foreshadowed the present pattern whereby the parishes of Darsham, Dunwich and Westleton are all served by the same parson living at Westleton.

Three parish clerks are mentioned in the parish registers: Braham Wolnough in 1699, and a Thomas Hill who, although not Darsham born, was certainly holding the office by 1796. He had married in Darsham in 1784 and had five children baptised here. Before he retired from this office in about

Darsham Old Hall

Darsham House

Views from the top of the church tower

The Nineteenth Century

1838, he had taken on as a deputy a young shoemaker by the name of William (Billy) Bezant. It is this parish clerk of whom we know a little more. Billy was born in Darsham in 1811, the eldest of the twelve children of John & Hannah Bezant. John Bezant was a shoemaker and had arrived in Darsham about 1810 and rented a property close to the church. The cottage now known as Orion Cottage was then known as Bezant's Cottage. Having learned his father's trade, Billy was appointed to the job of sexton and later took over as parish clerk. He held this post for 63 years until his death in 1901. He appears to have been somewhat of a character. He remained unmarried, the story goes, as after having courted his intended for twenty years, she then married someone else. The boys of the village would pick on Billy when they felt like annoying an adult, but his strong voice was to be heard leading the singing and responses at church services, and the Parish Report for 1891 tells of him entertaining upwards of forty old people of the village, when he sang a song at a supper held to commemorate his jubilee year as clerk. He was then in his eighty second year. Billy died in 1901 and was buried in the churchyard in the grave of his parents in March, and the office of parish clerk was abolished. The Vicar reported that:

> '...our old Parish Clerk, after holding office for nearly sixty-three years, was called away at the good old age of ninety: peaceable, quiet, ever ready and willing to oblige and always at his post till within two or three days of his death the

The Nineteenth Century

old man laid down his burden through sheer exhaustion of old age. He had of late become too feeble to be relied upon, and perhaps we may say with all respect he had outlived his usefulness.'

Billy was to be seen around the village, always dressed in a moleskin waistcoat, which it is said had cost seven shillings and sixpence, almost a whole week's wages at that time. He wore a cloth wrapper round his neck and a French hat, a small round braided hat with a flat top and a peak. Billy Bezant had stayed put in Darsham all his life: his world was Darsham. By contrast, newcomers were arriving in the village, and getting there by the newest form of transport.

In about 1885, James Black and his wife Janet hired a whole railway train to bring their family and the contents of their farm in Scotland to Darsham, where they took the tenancies of Whitehouse Farm and Priory Farm. There were ten children in the family aged 15 years and upwards. Things were better in Darsham than they were in Scotland! Two of the daughters subsequently married two Aldrich brothers, who were both farmers, born at Cratfield. The Black family were nonconformists and so too were the Aldrich family.

The first evidence of public Christian worship in Darsham outside the Anglican tradition comes from 1812 when a private house in Brussels Green was licensed for worship. There is similar evidence from 1830. Darsham has had a

The Primitive Methodist Chapel at the beginning of the 20th century & at the end

Mrs A. Aldrich opening the Sunday School extension to the Chapel in 1908

The Nineteenth Century

Primitive Methodist chapel since 1836. The first building was on the west side of Fox Lane. It was replaced by the present chapel in order to seat 120, on the east side of Fox Lane in 1873 at a cost of £229.11s.4d. In 1908 the chapel was extended at a cost of £65 to include a Sunday school room. In 1932 the Primitive Methodists became part of the new 'Methodist Church.'

About 1896, Mr Andrew Aldrich, a liberal by political persuasion and a Methodist by religion, had become the tenant farmer of Darsham Hall farm. The chapel is conveniently close to the farm. He naturally supported it, and he expected his employees to be seen at the chapel services on Sundays. Interestingly, the Aldrich brothers were claimed to be the first farmers in Darsham to send milk commercially to London by train. Meanwhile, Darsham House being at the parish church end of the village, and the Parry-Crooke family being firm patrons of the church, they expected their employees to be seen at the church services on Sundays. All this, it is said, on pain of losing their jobs and tied cottages.

The story goes that at Michaelmas, the time of hiring at the beginning of the farming year, The Street was alive with people moving house, with their possessions on handcarts. This practice is borne out by reference to baptisms in the church and chapel registers when, at times, families had several children baptised at both. Between the years of 1886 and 1912, the Black/Aldrich years at the chapel, there were

The Nineteenth Century

114 baptisms at the chapel and 130 at the parish church, indicating a degree of equipoise within the village. It should be acknowledged that Dr Tennant, as the vicar, was quite disconcerted to report that there was only one baptism at the parish church for the whole of 1899. However, this apparent competition for loyalty should not be inflated out of proportion as there have been around 3,400 baptisms recorded at the parish church, more than ten times the recorded number for the chapel.

The Parry-Crooke family is remembered by wall tablets in the parish church. They moved into Darsham House in 1877. They soon established their position as resident landlords, who were interested in the affairs of the village, and they maintained a squirearchical balance between interest and aloofness. They certainly had ways of ingratiating themselves with the people. From their earliest years in Darsham the Parry-Crookes gave a 'Servants' Ball' in early January for tenants, tradesmen, and others. There was dancing from 8pm to midnight, when there was a tremendous meal, followed by more dancing well into the small hours, and ending with rousing cheers for the hosts. In 1888 the eldest son of the Parry-Crookes brought his wife Georgiana to live at Darsham House. Georgiana Parry-Crooke was greatly respected by tenant farmers, estate workers, domestic staff and villagers for her unfailing kindness and generosity. Mothers with new babies were given a pram-set, children were given money on fête days. The children of the village were allowed to play on one of their lawns, with no

The Nineteenth Century

restriction as to the amount of noise that was generated. On Empire Day (24th May - Queen Victoria's birthday) they would entertain all the day-school children (sometimes as many as 80) to tea and games - the main feature of which was a pole, similar to a telegraph pole, with pieces of wood across the top, on which were nailed several bags of sweets. The children had to knock the bags down by throwing up balls! Georgiana only left Darsham in 1939 when she was widowed.

Around 1860, a collection was taken among the gentry, the vicar, and some of the farmers, towards the purchase of a harmonium at a cost of £21, to provide music for hymn singing. 'Hymns Ancient & Modern' was being published at this time, and brought a revolution in church music - including the music in Darsham Church. Lists of donors are a fascinating link with the past, and so much can be read into the list of supporters for the harmonium:

Earl of Stradbroke	£5. 0. 0d	Owner of Darsham Hall
A. Purvis	3. 3. 0d	Owner of Darsham House
F.J.P.Scrivner Esq.	3. 0. 0d	Tenant of Darsham House c.1864
Revd. T. Mayhew	2. 2. 0d	Vicar of Darsham 1851-1865
Col. Wm. Blois	1. 0. 0d	Darsham Cottage.
H. Thrupp Esq.	1. 1. 0d	of London
J. Thrupp Esq.	1. 1. 0d	of London
Mr Clutten	1. 0. 0d	Whitehouse Farm
Mr Smyth	6. 9d	The Miller
Mr Chilvers	10. 0d	Possibly of Priory Farm
R. Gorham	5. 0d	
Mr Huckman	2. 6d	Home Farm Brussels Green

Total £18.11.3d

The Nineteenth Century

Whilst Miss Laura Mountain was organist at the church from 1889 until 1909, we have no written evidence of a church choir before 1890 when the headmaster of the school was choirmaster until his transfer to Theberton in 1892. Rev. Tennant took over the job and within two years had formed a new choir of six men and six boys all resplendent in surplices. Over the next ten years, the numbers increased to ten men and ten boys under the guidance of a Mr C. Field and, later, of the then headmaster of the day school, Mr G.Ludbrooke. In 1903 Vicar Tennant complained about the publication of a new hymn book, expressing his frustration that if the whole Church of England used the same prayer book, the same hymn book (Ancient & Modern) should also be used throughout. To his credit, it has to be said, Vicar Tennant gradually changed his mind, and in 1912 the whole choir and congregation were provided with a new hymn book - 'Church Hymns'. As his life unfolded it emerged that it was not unusual for him to take some years to 'think things through' - no wonder he stayed at Darsham so long, it must have been a very congenial place for him to minister.

Until 1947 the church was lit by oil lamps. Towards the end of the nineteenth century subscriptions were invited to buy new lamps. Those who responded were:

D. Parry-Crooke	£2. 0. 0d	Anonymous	5s 0d
Mrs Parry-Crooke	1. 0. 0d	X.Y.Z. (sic)	5s 0d
Mrs W. Parry-Crooke	2. 0. 0d	Mrs Gould	5s 0d
Mrs Waterfield	10. 0d	A member	2s.6d
Mr & Mrs F.W.Brook	10. 0d	Miss Freeth	5s 0d

Darsham Church Choir in the 1920's
with the Rev. Dr Tennant

Darsham Church Choir 1944 - 1945
with Rev. Maitland

Darsham Church Choir 1950 - 1951
with Canon Lee

The Nineteenth Century

Mrs Arnott & family	12. 0d	Mr Bezant	2s 6d
"A friend"	10. 0d	Simon Bezant	2s 6d
The Vicar	10. 0d	"A friend"	3s 0d
"A friend"	5. 6d	Mr & Mrs Davis	3s 0d
Mr Simon Page	5. 0d	Jessie Dunnet	5s 0d
The Misses Lovett	5. 0d	Mr Roberts	5s 0d

£11. 1s.0d

Ten lamps were installed and hung on each side of the aisle in October 1898, having been purchased at a cost of £14, of which £11.1s.0d came from the subscriptions and the balance was made up from church funds. When the fund raising for the installation of electricity was under way in the 1940's, even more illustrious help was received. China and tablecloths were given to be prizes for a whist drive by the Dowager Queen Mary and the then Queen Elizabeth, but no one now knows who gave which, or where it all went to! A wealth of records from the nineteenth century have survived. Many gifts were given to the parish church by the parishioners. In 1861 we have a report of a new stove being placed at the west end of the church, for the comfort of the aged poor. In 1885 it was recorded in the Parish Report that a government grant of £5.10s.0d, together with 14s.6d from the Sunday school and £4.2s.0d from the evening school was given to the church towards the boarding of the floor, which had previously been of brick, in the open seats for the poor. The vicar wrote that he hoped that the poor would show their gratitude by using the seats.

The Nineteenth Century

The Annual Parish Reports of the Rev. Christopher Tennant tell us much about the church during his incumbency from 1889 to 1927, but they also tell us about the man himself. He did not always see eye-to-eye with his parishioners, proving to be confrontational at times. A report in the *Halesworth Times* for 7th April, 1891 gives us an idea of what it was like for the parish to adjust to its new vicar:

DARSHAM - VESTRY MEETING

'The proceedings at the Easter Vestry meeting were of a particular 'lively' character. The Vicar, the Revd. R.C. Tennant presided.

Before the proceedings commenced, Mr Henry Gunn, the Parish Warden, said that he wished to read out a letter which the Vicar had addressed to him - the Vicar said that he could not allow that; it was not before the meeting and it would not be in order to read it. - This statement was received with dissent, on which Mr Gunn asked those who wished the letter to be read to hold up their hands and this was done by the whole meeting, on which the Vicar said, 'Well it can be read, it's nothing I'm ashamed of.'

The letter was then read, as follows - 'As you have seen fit to absent yourself for some considerable time (without reference to me as Vicar) from the parish church of which you have been legally appointed Churchwarden, and have thus deliberately neglected those duties which the law requires you to perform, I hereby call upon you (as

Incumbent of the parish) to explain the reason for such conduct. Unless I have some explanation from you at once, I intend to write without delay to the Archdeacon for advice, which I am sure will make matters very unpleasant for you. You cannot expect one in my position to stand by and take no notice of your conduct which is a scandal to the Church and to the Parish and one which the law will by no means permit. If you wish to give up your office, do so in a straightforward manner and call a Vestry for the purpose of appointing another in your place, or give up your books and accounts into my hands with your written resignation and I will see to the appointment being made. Not only is your conduct in withdrawing from the active duties of your office reprehensible in the extreme, but in refusing also to attend to the repairs of the Church, shows you to be careless of those duties and thus not a fit person to undertake them. I may add, on this matter, that I have myself given orders for the work to be done which you refused to see to when spoken to this afternoon on the matter and it is necessary to say further that the bill will be presented for payment at Easter and we will see whether it will be a lawful item for settlement among the Churchwardens accounts at that time. The matter which compels me to write this letter cannot remain where it is and if the scandalous report which I have heard be true, viz., that you have been attending another parish church, you cannot be ignorant enough or unreasonable enough not to expect it. I therefore call upon you for an explanation and also to resume your duties at once, failing which I shall make my complaint to the Archdeacon and thus take legal proceedings. I expect you will be good enough to call upon me today and let me know your intentions.'

Mr Gunn (indignantly) - 'Now gentlemen, what do you think of a letter like that?, I say it is scandalous to write it.' The Vicar said it was the duty of the Churchwarden to attend the Parish Church, assist in keeping order in the Church, and seeing that no-one remained in the Churchyard during the service - Mr Gunn disputed that such were his duties and the argument proceeded warmly. In the course of it, Mr Gunn drew attention to an item in the accounts of ten shillings paid for what he called 'an old gown'. This, the Vicar explained was for the Parish Clerk and was in accordance with the injunction that all things should be done decently and orderly.

Reference was also made to a payment of four shillings to a policeman, who had been employed, the Vicar said, to keep order in the Churchyard, which was Mr Gunn's duty. Incidentally, a parishioner, asked 'What was this scandal Mr Gunn had raised in the parish?' Mr Gunn answered, 'In leaving his Church to hear a better man'. The Vicar then said that he would bow his head in acknowledgement of a better man than himself and then expounded the duties of a Churchwarden.

The conversation was prolonged for some time and Mr Johnson said that he attended the Church but did not hear the Gospel - 'you preach at us but do not preach the Gospel', he said. The Vicar said, 'I did not come here to be taught my duty.' A long discussion then took place as to the registration fee of ten shillings which had not been paid, Mr Gunn saying that he had not the money. In the end, the Vicar signed the accounts which were passed, adding a note that the registration fee was not paid for want of funds.

Mr Gunn was re-elected Parish Warden, with thanks for past services - Mr Johnson remarked that he had performed his duties to the satisfaction of the whole parish. Mr Parry-Crooke was nominated Vicar's Warden.'

The feeling that the vicar had to come up to the expectations of the congregation was an interesting stimulus to the life of the village. These were probably very unhappy years for Vicar Tennant. He had arrived in 1889, and in the first five years he buried his wife and a daughter. The very vulnerable vicar felt betrayed by one of his churchwardens, Mr Gunn, who was accused of going to another parish church. The desire to 'hear the Gospel' raises the question as to what the gospel was thought to be at that time and in that circle. The answer came ten years later.

Vicar Tennant remarried in 1895. Together with the local gentry, the vicar and his wife were to become the mainstay of the parish, organising the welfare of the villagers. Several parish funds had been set up by the Rev. and Mrs Thorpe and were continued by Rev. & Mrs Tennant. A Clothing and Shoe Club first recorded in 1880, provided a premium for savers of 2d to 4d per week to provide for boots; the Tea Club commenced in 1901 for the bulk purchase of tea producing a saving of 2d per pound for those whose payments

The Nineteenth Century

of 2d to 6d per week were to fund the outlay. The Coal Fund was a charitable fund raised and paid for by the local gentry from proceeds of concerts and lectures, with the aim of providing coal at half-price to the poor, the widows and the needy of the parish. Most of these funds were only wound up at the end of World War I.

The impression of Darsham at the end of the nineteenth century is of a busy and industrious place. The railway had come in the 1850's, and the station had a growing importance for local farmers and visitors. However, the century ended with a degree of a lack of self-confidence within the Anglican Church. A book called 'Our Empty Churches: the cause and the remedy' was published in 1899, thus giving the lie to any facile inflated claims for Victorian church attendance. In Darsham, local well-being still depended on hard work and the favour of the principal employers of the parish, but there was a rising sense of well-being and prosperity. The century ended with a midnight celebration of the Holy Communion in the parish church at which nineteen parishioners received the sacrament. There was still poverty, but there was hope.

Chapter Seven

The Twentieth Century

An item of national importance which involved every citizen, man, woman and child, was the death of Queen Victoria in January, 1901. A memorial service was held in Darsham church, reported by the *East Anglian Daily Times* on 4th February, 1901. The Revd. Dr Tennant, the vicar at the time, conducted the special form of service. The passing bell was muffled and at the close of the service, the 'Dead March' in Saul was played.

In the years immediately before and after 1900 the Church Army Mission van with its Captain Smith and Cadet Gravett, would arrive in the village for a visit once a year, staying for about two weeks. They conducted services and prayer meetings which were very well attended; they sold books and pamphlets for the furtherance of their work, and they presented the Sunday school prizes. To those who attended the services they issued signed cards as mementoes of their visit. The Rev. Tennant was always well satisfied with their work which encouraged more people to regular church attendance. The visits usually ended with the Sunday school pupils and their parents being entertained to tea on the Vicarage lawn.

Darsham Vicarage was built about 1870 and the following record of its sale appeared in the *East Anglian Daily Times,* 8th December, 1971.

'The Vicarage ...... Late Victorian - resembles the

work of William Pattisson, a Woodbridge architect, who died in 1878. He also designed Bawdsey Rectory which is similar. The present incumbent is the Revd. Jas. Lovejoy. The house has not been lived in for about 2 years.'

The sale of the vicarage was completed in February, 1972, to Mr C. Somerville who renamed it 'The Old Rectory'. Possibly he thought it an improvement, but it was rather inappropriate as we have never had a Rector. The house was sold again in 1985 to Mr Michael Potter, an artist, who resold the property in 1989 to Mr Michael Peters, the present owner. Mr Potter refurbished the house and added a studio wing over the garages during his occupation. It is said by staff who worked in the house early in the century that the vicarage is haunted by the apparition of a woman, referred to as the Grey Lady who was claimed to walk down the staircase, out of the front door and across to the church, but there have been no suggestions concerning who this lady might be or how the story originated. Possibly this story began as a way of ensuring that young servants did not loiter in the main part of the house.

No mention has been made yet of the village school: a key provision for the well-being of the young. In 1901, there were about 72 children in the school, aged 4 to 14 years. The school had been purpose built in 1854 at a cost of £80. The sequence of school log books begins in 1877. The school had many changes of head teacher until 1893 when Mr

The Church Army Van
outside the gates of
Darsham house c.1900

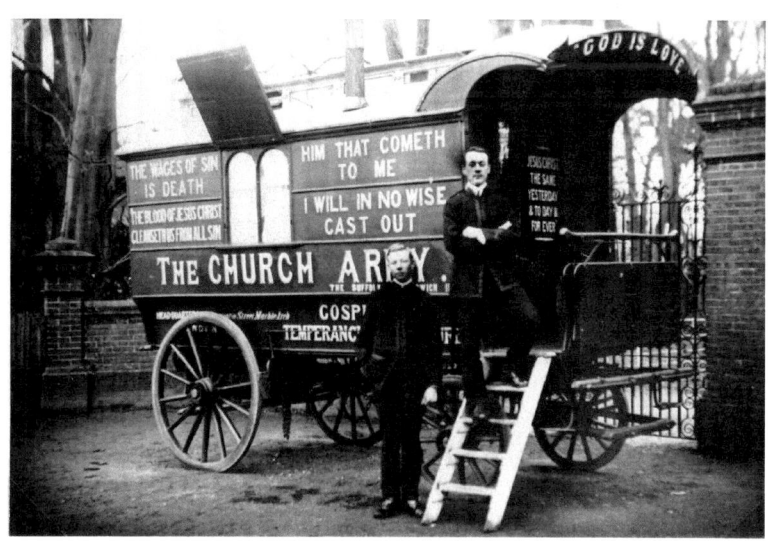

**Sunday School outings
with Rev. Tennant
c.1895 & in 1919**

The Twentieth Century

and Mrs Ludbrook arrived. They remained until 1925 and appear to have been excellent teachers, exerting a good influence on the children in their care. Staff then kept changing until 1933 when Mrs Elsie Quadling arrived, who was headmistress until her death in 1954. She was followed by Mrs Joan Weaver who was the last headmistress when the school closed, there being only 12 remaining pupils, in 1966. The school was sold for £2,400 in 1968. The highest number of children ever recorded in the school had been in 1881 when there were 94 children crammed into the little school.

Vicar Tennant had moments when he could be prophetic. In 1908 he warned parents to send their children to Sunday school:

> '... before long all church schools will be forcefully submerged and state school will prevail throughout the kingdom. These schools will be state schools giving state education, taking no cognizance of religious education and church teaching will be ousted from the curriculum.'

Later in the century, the following comment was published in the *Church Times*: 'The increase of crime among juveniles is almost entirely due to the cessation of definite religious instruction in the schools'. It may come as a surprise that this comment was printed in September, 1923, and may be grounds for anxiety as we reflect on this matter seventy seven years later.

The Twentieth Century

Dr Tennant was clearly interested in the history of Darsham, and he also looked back through the old registers. He wrote to *The Halesworth Times* on 21st May, 1901 recounting the entries that he had found relating to the generosity of the little village so many years before:

'I referred you some time ago to the interesting records to be found in many of our old parish registers, where, for instance is one of which I think will be of special interest to your readers in Halesworth; it points to a time when a great calamity befell the town, and when the parish of Darsham came to its relief: of a time when the larger and richer parish did not hesitate to accept kindly help from a smaller and poorer neighbour, being kindly offered: it is an instance too, Sir, now becoming rare, of the sympathy and close connexion which existed between neighbouring parishes when they were not quite so 'Congregationalist' as they are fast becoming in these days. But let the Record speak for itself: '1674 - collected for the relief of the poor of Halesworth, when visited by the small-pox £10.7s.9d.' This was no mean sum to be collected in a parish like Darsham, nor, indeed would many a larger parish Church today consider such a sum unworthy of its own congregation. However, it affords a lesson to all of us Parsons and Parishes alike - the duty of coming forward to help each other in trouble and disasters *social*, as well as in the longer and so called more important matters called *Religious*. Sir, nothing is religious but the law of Christ - bear ye one another's burdens and so fulfil the law of Christ.'

The Church c. 1910 & The School

School Children c. 1895-1900
& in 1959, a few years before
the school closed.

The Twentieth Century

This was quite an important letter. It was Dr Tennant's way of resolving the challenge that the same newspaper had identified 10 years beforehand from that very contentious Vestry Meeting. Dr Tennant had been accused of not preaching the gospel, now he felt confident to declare what he saw the gospel to be in Darsham at that time: *'bear ye one another's burdens and so fulfil the law of Christ'*. Dr Tennant's ministry blossomed. An example of his style can be traced in the report (*Halesworth Times* - 24th October, 1905) of a special service for the centenary of the death of Admiral Nelson at the Battle of Trafalgar in 1805:

'The Nelson Centenary was observed with due enthusiasm and spirit at Darsham Church on Saturday and Sunday last. The two ensigns, Naval and Mercantile Marine together with the Union Jack were hoisted over the tower where they floated bravely in the breeze. At half past four, the hour of Nelson's death, these were taken down and the Union Jack hoisted at half mast and the church bell solemnly tolled for half an hour. Inside the church was decorated with English flags from one end to the other whilst a large oil painting of Lord Nelson was set over against the pulpit; over the front entrance of the church floated the Red Ensign.

There were three sermons on Sunday - Dr Tennant, the Vicar gave three addresses on the character, the deeds and the death of the great Admiral. In the afternoon, every boy and girl was made to repeat the famous words of Nelson - 'I will be a Hero, the Lord being my helper,' and

The Twentieth Century

at the close of the service, every one present was presented with a sprig of the old yew tree (Nelson's tree) still growing in the churchyard of Burnham Thorpe, the parish where Horatio Nelson was born.

Larger congregations than usual filled the church, who fully entered into the enthusiasm and spirit of the occasion. At the end of the service, the National Anthem was sung and the 'Dead March' in Saul played on the organ whilst the congregation stood in silent homage to a great memory and in devout sympathy for the passing of the greatest hero in English history.'

Village suppers were quite a regular event as shown in the following item in the *Halesworth Times* - 3rd May, 1904:

'A supper, given by the congregation of Darsham Parish Church to all the old people of the age of 65 years and upwards, took place in the Schoolroom, on Friday evening. Twenty-nine out of a total of thirty-seven invited sat down and enjoyed a very hearty and pleasant meal. After the supper, whilst the old men were enjoying their pipes and ale, an entertainment took place, presided over by Mr J. Norton, Churchwarden. The following assisted: Mrs Norton, Messrs Simpson Bros., Miss Arnott, Miss Fisher, Miss Tennant, the Rev. Dr Tennant.'

In the early years of the 20th century, there were annual outings for the choir and the Sunday school, often taken jointly and usually to Dunwich by horses and wagons provided by the local farmers, but occasionally, as in 1904, the choir spent a day in Great Yarmouth. We find that in 1916, the choirboys and Sunday school scholars, together with their teachers, took their annual outing at Aldeburgh, going by wagonette, the total cost of the outing being £2.7s.6d. The chapel organised similar but separate outings.

Occasionally, special services were held for cyclists. Cycling was becoming an enjoyable and regular pass-time - certainly it was one of Vicar Tennant's interests. The Cyclists Touring Club had initially been formed in Yorkshire in 1878. By 1880 there were already 230 clubs in the United Kingdom, and the popularity of cycling continued to grow. *'Letts's Cycling Map of England and Wales'* was first printed in 1884. Darsham church could be packed with cyclists from far and wide and a report from *The Halesworth Times* - 27th October, 1908 reads:

CYCLISTS' CHURCH PARADE

'A special service for cyclists was held in Darsham Church on Sunday and in spite of the threatening aspect of the weather, a large company assembled, there being upwards of 150 cyclists (ladies and gentlemen) present. This being the first occasion of such a service, great interest was shown and the sight of all those bicycles stored against the old church was exceedingly striking. At the conclusion of the service, large numbers turned out to see the departure of their guests. The service was fully choral, with hymns processional and recessional under

The Twentieth Century

the leadership of Mr Field, the Choirmaster. Dr Tennant, the Vicar, preached from Ecclesiastes xi, 9 - 'Rejoice O young men in your youth'. The cyclists present were very gratified at the invitation and the service, many of them expressing the hope that they might be repeated again next year.'

At another such service it was reported that the mayor of Beccles read the lessons.

On 18th April, 1912, a memorial service was held after the report of the sinking of the Titanic when the offertory of £5 was donated to the relief of the bereaved relatives.

Dr Tennant's ministry in Darsham ended in 1927 when he retired to Hampshire. He died there in 1943 aged 91.

During this century there has been much restoration of the church. The porch had been renewed in 1887 at a cost of £40, commemorating the Golden Jubilee of Queen Victoria. The thatched roof of the porch was replaced with tiles in 1904, and in the same year, Mr Mountain, the builder, was contracted to remove the old lead from the south side of the main roof of the church and replace it with tiles and to add the stone cross. Part of the cost of his bill of £45.2s.6d was raised by selling the old lead for £38.15s.0d, the remaining sum being made up from offertory collections.

The years of Edward VII saw many minor changes in the church. A Casson Positive Organ was installed at a cost of

The Twentieth Century

£101. It was dedicated in August 1903. This was the first pipe organ in Darsham Church. It would have sounded much more grand than the harmonium which it replaced. In Darsham nothing is thrown away if it can be avoided, and the old harmonium was converted in the 1960's by Mr John Moody into a chest for storage. The money for the new pipe organ, its particular brand being described as the 'best organ for small churches', was raised by subscription, by monthly silver offertories, and by musical concerts. Originally placed on the right in the chancel, it obstructed the view of the altar for those seated on the right hand side of the nave. By 1947 this organ had come to the end of its days and a new organ was installed. The organ was rebuilt at the back of the church in its present position in 1973.

In 1905 a new oak lectern was presented by Mr D Parry-Crooke together with a new bible in memory of the late James Langley Tennant, eldest son of the vicar, who died and was buried at sea in March of that year. In 1907 an oak screen was designed and made by John Martin & Sons of Darsham. It encloses the tower arch and entrance to the belfry and forms a vestry. It was built at a cost of £14.11s.3d. The communion rails were designed by J. Norton, churchwarden, and made by the Martin family and installed at Christmas 1909 at a cost of £12.1s.6d. This sum had been raised in the parish by subscription. In 1912, the oak canopy for the font was also made by the Martin family, to mark the coronation of George V. A member of the Martin family, Miss Sally Martin, died in 1977 having been village postmistress for many years. Three of her nephews were involved in creating a lasting memorial to her in the form of our splendid churchyard gates. Mr Jack Martin designed the gates, Mr Michael Shipp made them, and Mr Harry Martin carved and erected them.

The appalling tragedy of the First World War invaded Darsham. Darsham servicemen were all remembered when bibles, prayer books and hymn books were included in parcels of comforts sent to them from the village. At the start of the First World War, vicar Tennant resolved that he would not miss a service or take a holiday until the war was over. He felt that he should be among his parishioners at such a sad time. He arranged for the Midday Bell to be rung each day, as a reminder to everyone in the village to offer prayers at the same moment. This practice was common in many towns and villages throughout the country. But from 1915 there was nobody free to ring the bell at Darsham.

In the latter part of 1914, a group of Darsham girls began to meet together under the leadership of Miss Constable, the housekeeper at Darsham Cottage. They were known as the Busy Bees and, with Miss Constable as Queen Bee, their express aim was knitting socks, scarves and mittens to which they added boot laces, a handkerchief, note paper, postcards, pencils, cigars and matches, and some small items of foodstuffs to be made into parcels to be sent to each of the Darsham men fighting for 'King & Country' - all of which was paid for by sales of work and proceeds of fêtes. They also collected eggs to send to Halesworth Hospital and made garments for the Ipswich Depot of the Red Cross.

The Church Organ before
& after its removal from the
Chancel to the back of the nave

The Altar rails made by the Martin Family In 1909

Dedication of the Martin Memorial Gates 1980.
Miss Alice Martin, Michael Shipp, Jack & Henry Martin.

The Twentieth Century

The boys of the village began to realise that they were being left out of doing their bit for the war effort, and in 1917 the Rev. Tennant organised the boys into a companion group which he named the Active Ants, and as leader he was known as the Master Ant. This band consisted of boys who pledged themselves to be useful according to their capacity to run errands and do odd jobs for a small sum around the parish. The boys were given a small collecting box and chose which war fund should benefit from their efforts.

The Roll of Honour of those who went to war was presented to the church in 1918. The brass cross for the altar is inscribed 'In memory of those who gave their lives for the freedom of the world, The Great War 1914-1919'. This was a gift from Georgiana Parry-Crooke and her husband. At the western end of the church, between the main gates and the church tower, stands the War Memorial originally dedicated to the sixteen Darsham servicemen who died in the First World War. Their record is probably typical of many villages: *Brigade Sgt. Maj. Charles Stammers* was one of the first Darsham men to be killed in action. He died in Belgium, November, 1914. *Sgt. Fred Lame* had left Darsham some years before and had made his home in Australia. He was seriously wounded in the Boer War. He volunteered in 1914 and came over with the Australian troops. He was wounded in the Dardanelles and died in May, 1915, in Malta. *Pte Lionel Parry-Crooke* fell in France July, 1916. The tale of loss cut through the village: *Pte Victor Balls* and *Pte Harold Balls, Pte Herbert James, Pte Herbert Geater, Sgt Fred Hambling, Gnr Harry Hambling,*

Sgt John Last, Seaman Arthur Runnacles, for all of these men some record is held as to where and when they died. No information is available as to the fate of *Capt. Gerald Brooke, Sgt. Charles Denny, Pte Robert Bishop, Gnr Horace Hart*, and *Arthur Mead*. Small wonder that a special service was held in the church in 1917 to celebrate America joining the cause of the Allies and a letter of appreciation was sent by the vicar, from the village, to the President of the United States. Altogether it is thought that 75 men of Darsham went off to the war. 16 died. The marble war memorial cross, which had been shipped from Italy earlier in the year, was unveiled by Mrs Parry-Crooke at a service in June, 1920.

Now note must be taken of the churchyard and the new burial ground. The work of digging graves usually fell to the sexton. He was also meant to keep the church clean and ring the bell, really acting as an assistant to the parish clerk. The names of some of our sextons and a little information about them has survived:

Edward Smith who died in Darsham in 1765 aged 72.
Thomas Curtis who died in 1770.
John Button who was born at Middleton. He was a farm labourer and lived at Sand Pit Cottage (Gravel Pit) next to Darsham Common and died in Darsham in 1800 aged 80.
Stephen Balls who was a gamekeeper. Born in Darsham in 1849, he married a Darsham girl and brought up thirteen children. The

Children of the Village c.1900
&
The Darsham Busy Bees 1914-1918

Elsie Hacon.
Confirmation Candidate
1st October, 1920.

NAMES ON THE ROLL OF HONOUR IN THE CHURCH W.W.I

BALLS B.E.S. - Pte. Suffolk Yeo.
BALLS E.P. - Cpl. A.S.C
BALLS H.P. - Pte.King's Liverpool Regt.
BALLS S.A. - Pte. Suffolk Regt.
BALLS V.C.J. - Pte. Suffolk Regt.
BALLS W.R. - M.T. A.S.C.
BALLS W.S. - H.M.S.Eglantine
BENSTEAD M. - Pte. Suffolk Yeo.
BISHOP R.J. - Pte. London Regt.
BISHOP R. - Pte. Grenadier Guards
BRABBIN H.C. - Pte. Sfk Regt.
BROOKE G.D. - Capt.Sfk Regt.
CATCHPOLE R.J. - Capt. Sfk Regt.
CRISP C. - Pte. Suffolk Regt.
CRISP D. - Pte. Royal Marines
CRISP J. - Gnr. R.F.A.
CRISP W. - Gnr. R.G.A.
DENNY A.E. - Sgt. R.F.A.
DENNY C.W. - Sgt. R.G.A.
FLEGG J. - E.Surrey Regt..
FLEGG Jas. - Pte. Suffolk Regt.
FLEGG T. - Pte.R.E.
FLEGG T. - Pte. Suffolk Regt.
FULLER W. Sgt. R.G.A.
GEATER W.S. - Spr. R.E.
GEATER A.G. - Pte. M.G.
GEATER H.T. - Pte. R.F.A
GOOCH M.J.M. - Pte.Royal Ssx.Rgt.
GOODCHILD A.F. - Pte. Sfk Regt.
GREEN H. - Pte. Suffolk Regt.
GREEN G. - H.M.Trawler Ferens
HAMBLING G. - Pte. Sfk Regt.
HAMBLING H. - Gnr. R.G.A.
HAMBLING F.C. - Sgt. R.G.A.
HART F. - Tpr. C.L.H.
HART H. - Gnr. R.G.A.
HICKFORD H.A. - Sgt.Middx. Regt.
HICKFORD W.J. - L.Cpl. M.G.C.
JAMES A. - H.M.S. Red Gauntlet
JAMES B. - Pte. Suffolk Regt.

JAMES C. - Pte. M.G.C.
JAMES W. - Pte. Essex Regt.
KNIGHTS G. - Cpl. R.H.A.
LAME F. - Sgt.Australian Army
LAME J. - H.M.S.Kessingland
LUDBROOKE F.C. - Lt.W.African Frontier Force
LUDBROOKE G.C. - Pte. RAMC
MANNING A.W. - Dvr. R.F.A.
MARTIN G.A. - L.Cpl. R.E.
MARTIN M. - L.Cpl. M.F.P.
MARTIN R. - Pte. Middx. Regt.
MAYHEW A. - Tpr.1st Life Guards
MAYHEW G. - Sgt.Maj. R.F.A.
MAYHEW H. - Gnr. R.F.A.
MAYHEW W. - Pte.Royal W.Kent Regt
NOLLER A.C. - L.Cpl. R.E.
NORMAN H.A. - Pte. Wwks.Regt.
PARRY-CROOKE C.P. - Capt.Sfk Regt.
PARRY-CROOKE L.W. Pte.Royal Fusiliers
PUNCHARD A.W.- H.M.S.Blenheim
ROBINSON H. - Cpl. M.F.P.
RUNNACLES A. - H.M.S. SPEY
RUNNACLES B. - Dvr. R.F.A.
RUNNACLES W. - Rfn.Rifle Bgde
SILLETT J. - Pte. Labour Corps.
SMITH A. - R.A.F.
SMITH C.W. - Bdr. R.G.A.
SMITH S.C. - Pte. Suffolk Regt.
STAMMERS .S - C. Sgt. Maj. W.O.R.F.A
TAYLOR J.W. - Gnr. R.G.A.
TENNANT A. - Chief Officer M.S.
TENNANT C. - Gnr. R.G.A.
TENNANT F.O. - 2nd Lt.Indian Army
THORNHILL N.M.C. Lt.Gren.Gds
TODD R.E. - Pte.Queens Royal W.Sry

The Dedication of the War Memorial 27th June 1920

The Twentieth Century

girls long outlived their brothers, one surviving to the age of 103.

George Meadows who was born at Worcester. He was a railway porter at the station and was sexton from 1906 to 1914. He died in Melton Asylum and was buried in Darsham in 1917.

Miles Martin   Darsham born, was a carpenter and joiner, who with his father did much of the carpentry that we see in the church today.

Alfred Hart   became sexton in 1918 when the annual salary for the appointment was £2.5s.0d. Alfred Hart was also Licensee of the Fox.

There have been about 1750 burials in the churchyard since the recording of burials in the parish registers began in 1539. Considering that the population before then would have been only in double figures, we might estimate some 3,000 burials in the churchyard during the millennium. Although we step down into the church, it has not been sinking, rather the level of the churchyard has slowly risen over the years. In March, 1917 the parish council were faced with the need for a new burial ground as the churchyard was reported to be so full that human remains were being unearthed whilst new graves were being dug. In the north wall of the chancel, on the outside, there is evidence of an aperture, now bricked up, which is believed to have been a bone-hole. Here bones were deposited that had been unearthed during the digging of new graves.

The Twentieth Century

Now, the vicar had a rose garden beside the churchyard, across the road from his house. This small parcel of land had once been known as the 'Thousand Acre' field - a typical piece of local humour. A deputation from the council consisting of Mr Parry-Crooke, the chairman, and two farmers approached Dr. Tennant for an extension to the churchyard. They reported back to the council that their suggestion that the vicar might offer a piece of the vicarage garden abutting the churchyard had been refused. However, the vicar wrote to offer a small field on Brussels Green, or a portion of the meadow adjoining the vicarage (the present Glebe Field). The council considered both of these plots to be unsuitable for the purpose and contacted the Rev. Scrimgeour of Sibton, the rural dean, asking for his assistance in the settlement of the matter. If an agreement was not forthcoming in the near future, the council had decided to approach the Home Office for an official Closure Order on the churchyard and to put into force the Burial Act requiring the provision of a cemetery. A month later, after efforts made by the Rural Dean, there was no agreement with the vicar and the Council wrote to the Home Office citing incidents and dates when human remains were thrown up whilst new graves were being dug and requesting information on the provision of an extension to the burial ground.

Nearly a year elapsed with still no solution and the council again contacted the vicar to ask what he was doing about the problem and at the June meeting of 1918 the council were able to report that the vicar had agreed to give up a plot 25 x 30 yards at the northern end of his garden which adjoined the

The Twentieth Century

churchyard. The council accepted. In December, 1919 a conveyance was completed and signed and the plot was soon in use. The remaining piece of that land was given over to the church for a future extension to the burial ground in 1953. In 1986 this further piece of land was prepared in the proper manner and it was consecrated by the Bishop of Dunwich in July, 1987. Since 1920, when the new burial ground was opened, there have been about 370 burials, the original plot has been filled and the remaining plot is in use. Until the late 1930s, funeral coffin bearers carried the coffin from the home to the church, but by then the village had expanded and it became quite a burden to carry from outlying properties. Sometimes considerable refreshments had to be supplied on the way. The village subscribed to purchase a bier which solved the problem. Motor hearses succeeded the bier which is now preserved in an outhouse at Darsham House. *(Note: In 2008, the bier was restored and is now displayed in the Church).*

On 8th May, 1977, to commemorate the Silver Jubilee of Queen Elizabeth II, an oak tree was planted in the churchyard and a plaque placed at it foot. On All Saints' Day, 1st November, 1992, to commemorate the 40 years of the reign of Queen Elizabeth II, holly trees were planted round the border of the churchyard by members of the parish, with a promise to look after them on at least four occasions annually, one of which would be on the birthday of its planter. To date most of the trees are flourishing.

After the long ministry of Vicar Tennant, note should be taken of Rowland Maitland (vicar 1933-1947), and Charles

The Twentieth Century

Waller (vicar 1954-1967). It was given to Vicar Maitland to be with the parish through the anxieties of the years of the Second World War. These were years when the station at Darsham could be extraordinarily busy with the arrival and departure of trainloads of soldiers involved in training at the battle school on the other side of Westleton and airmen from the local R.A.F. Station. Yet again, young men of Darsham were caught up in a global conflict.

The radar towers on the High Street kept watch. These towers, known as the 'Darsham Pylons', stood for 20 years. There were four steel masts that were each 360 feet high, and four wooden masts of 240 feet. They towered over the countryside and their use quickly became a subject for speculation. The general opinion was that they were a form of 'Death Ray' and inventive minds elaborated upon this. One theory originated from the driver of a car whose vehicle inexplicably stopped on the A12. He blamed it on the 'pylons' which he declared must be there to stop the engines of German aircraft - it stood to reason! It only took another driver to report, truthfully or not, that he too had had the same experience for the theory to pass into fact. So, the 'Darsham Pylons' entered Suffolk folklore, and were regarded with mild trepidation by motorists who were quite relieved to pass by without incident. In fact, the 'Darsham Pylons' was really RAF High Street, one of the first operational radar stations in the world. The equipment detected aircraft at a distance of up to 300 miles.

It is thought that 34 men of Darsham went off to the Second

Baptism & Burial facilities

The 15$^{th.C}$ Font with a 20$^{th.C}$ Cover.

&

The 20$^{th.C}$ Bier.

A Cottage which was previously two, belonging to the Town Trust.

An aerial view of the Church & its surroundings.

The Twentieth Century

World War. The names of the four men who never returned were added to the War Memorial, they were: *David Holmes* who died in the sinking of H.M.S. Hood; *Percy Stammers* died, but it is not known where; *John Rouse* died in the service of the merchant navy at sea; *William Watling* died serving in the Far East. The end of the war was not the end of the service of men from Darsham - *William Nunn* joined the Palestine Police in February, 1947. These were very turbulent times and in September, 1947, he was killed and buried at Haifa.

In an alcove in the parish church, in front of the roll of honour, stands the ship's bell from H.M.S. Darsham. The name of this ship arose as a tribute to the school children and Mrs Quadling, the headmistress of Darsham School, who sent comforts to the Royal Navy during the war. After the war, by way of gratitude, a small ship was named H.M.S. Darsham and stationed in Hong Kong, patrolling in the Far East. When this ship was decommissioned the bell was presented to the parish and handed over at a ceremony in July, 1966. It was most fitting that the vicar receiving the bell should have been Rev. Waller. He had served as a chaplain in the Royal Navy 1910-1928.

One of the many organisations of which records have survived from the time of Mr Waller's incumbency is the Mothers' Union. In February, 1956 they took advantage of a popular format and hosted an 'Any Questions' meeting in the WI Hut. This was an open meeting with a good attendance, including a party from Theberton. The questions were

The Twentieth Century

recorded, but not the deliberations of the panel, and survive as a window on the things that were being discussed 45 years ago. The questions were:

1) What is the team's opinion of the fact that a church in Ipswich has banned coloured people from its congregation?
2) Do 'Horror Comics' present any problem in England?
3) Does the team agree with the saying: 'Spare the rod and spoil the child'?
4) Will the team give their opinion on the 'Abolition of Hanging'?
5) Should parents leave small children alone in order to get to work?
6) Is it right for boys of 19 to fight in any war zone when they cannot vote until they are 21?
7) Why is it so difficult to get young mothers to join the M.U.?

These questions took about an hour to discuss. Probably current versions of these questions would take about as long to discuss today, and much of the agenda to these questions will be present in our spectrum of concern in the future. Meanwhile, it is good to know that a village that has always relied so heavily on 'incomers' for its population kept looking outward. It was typical that Darsham even responded to the troubles of Hungary in 1956. According to the minute books of the Mothers' Union arrangements were planned for a social to be held in December, 1956 in support of the Hungarian Relief Fund.

There was a church Sunday school until Rev. Waller's time. In the 30's, before the war, Sunday school outings were by Eastern Counties Bus to Southwold. Tea was at Jackson's Restaurant above what is now Denny's shop in the Market

Ship's Bell from H.M.S. DARSHAM

**Palm Sunday Service with the donkey
1990**

**Freddie Flegg & Ruth Kerridge
Past Churchwardens, Bellringers
& P.C.C. Members**

**Some members of the
Darsham P.C.C. - 1991**

The Twentieth Century

Place. The amusements at the pier were visited, and the small shop where souvenirs were bought is still there. Mention must also be made of the robed choir which was greatly built up under Rev. Maitland and which numbered 21 in 1944-1945, and which reached 32 in 1950-1951. This was a great local asset, and brought people together in a special way. Mrs Fisk of Westleton was organist in the late 1940's. Mr Elystan Phillips was organist for some years until 1983.

In the last decade of the century the restoration of the tower was made possible by contributions totalling £26,781 raised by the parish. This was a huge amount of money to be found from a parish of less than 300 people, and the response was amazing. It is very pleasing to record that Westleton and Dunwich PCC's both assisted. Grants from church trusts and a state aided grant allowed the completion of extensive restoration work to the tower which was completed in 1991 at a total cost of nearly £62,000. The workmen who executed these repairs were: D. (Spike) Bloomfield and D. Keeble, both of Debenham, and M. Clements of Coddenham.

The relaying of the floor was undertaken in 1996, the brickwork being largely done by Brian Sillett of Upper Weybread. Much of the recent work of repairs and renewals of the woodwork of the church has been carried out by a local craftsman, Ronnie Gallant. This includes the reconstruction of the pulpit which was found to have been unlikely to survive any weighty preaching. The Vicar was gleefully assured that the only thing that had been supporting him in

The Twentieth Century

the centre of the pulpit had been a small piece of carpet. Since the repair of the pulpit it is said that sermons have been considerably lengthened. Currently, the PCC is working towards the removal of the rendering on the outside of the south wall in an attempt to solve the damp problems on the inside.

Darsham PCC had been constituted in 1920. The earliest surviving minute books that have been traced began in 1950. Vicar Waller retired in 1967, and the living was suspended - which basically meant that no new appointment was to be made until decisions had been taken on the future pattern of ministry in the area. Rev. Lovejoy, the Vicar of Westleton, was asked to take pastoral care of the parish whilst extensive discussions took place. Despite the anxieties of the PCC, in 1971 Darsham was joined as an ecclesiastical parish to be held in plurality with Westleton & Dunwich by Vicar James Lovejoy. A most memorable village fête was held in 1974 before his retirement. At that fête there was a 'buy-a-tile' stall, which helped to finance Mr Reg Spindler's work replacing the lead on the north side of the nave roof. The inscriptions on the lead were cut out to be displayed in the church but, curiously, there was a slight delay of about 20 years before this actually happened. The next two vicars were Ian Robinson (1974-1984) and Richard Ginn (1985-). In January, 1995, a thanksgiving service was held to commemorate the centenary of the inauguration of the first Darsham Parish Council, and the vicar cast some thoughts upon village life in his sermon.

The Twentieth Century

During this history, considerable reference has been made to the vicars of the parish. This is inevitable as they have had to represent so many concerns, hopes, and needs. Tapestry kneelers to commemorate the long list of vicars of Darsham were worked by the following friends of All Saints' Church between 1972 & 1975:

Mona Allen	Jean Zonczyk-Bohusz	Marjorie Campbell
Gwen Carter	Hazel Crane	Nickey Crane
Hilda Cruickshank	Hope Sanger	Blanche Feilden
Gladys Jackson	Doreen Lovejoy	Alice Martin
Sally Martin	Nancie Moody	Mary Stephenson
Katharine Mitchell	Sarah O'Connor	Hilda Rawlins
Peggy Youell	Eirene Rodocanachi	Clare Sanger
Cynthia Rodocanachi	Anita Smith	Joan Spindler

The threads of history weave together. Many names of those who have made Darsham what it is have been lost, and so little is known about many of the names that have been preserved, but all the people who have ever lived in Darsham have contributed to make the village what it is today. Looking around our little parish church, with its pleasant churchyard, it is difficult to imagine the total activity of the last thousand years, out of which approximately 1,750 burials, 3,400 baptisms and more than 850 marriages have actually been recorded. The true total numbers will never be known.

Village organisations have come and gone. Whilst the Village today enjoys the Women's Institute, the Mothers' Union, Friday Club, the Horticultural Society, and Carpet

The Twentieth Century

Bowls, there were also: Evergreen's Club, Old Comrade's Association, Football, Cricket, Quoits, Darts, Girl Guides, Boy Scouts, the Band of Hope Union, and the Christian Endeavour Society - all of which helped to give guidance and recreation to the population. Darsham has always been a community that has had to make its own amusements. In a small place things only happen if people contribute their time and their talents, their enthusiasm and their initiative. For some years, the chapel ran the only Sunday school in the village. This closed in 1998, and a party was held and presentations were made to Lilian Dunnett and Sister Rose Boulton in gratitude for their marvellous long service.

A transformation in the character of the village that has taken place over this century is that the village has come to be a place where people choose to come and live. Some may first arrive as holidaymakers, or buy a property in anticipation of retirement. But Darsham is now definitely a place to which to come rather than a place from which to get away.

On a small table by the door into the church is a Visitors' Book in which visitors are invited to sign their names and to add a comment if they wish. Reading this book, we can see that many people who visit and sign the book are holidaymakers and their comments confirm the feelings of the parishioners, that this is a beautiful and peaceful church. However, others who sign have a very close connection with our church: those who were baptised here; those who were married here. People return not only to see the changes, but perhaps to remember happy days in Darsham. There is also

The Twentieth Century

another group of visitors who come to look at Darsham Church and absorb the atmosphere that nurtured their forebears.

The century began with Vicar Tennant expounding the gospel in terms of a quotation from St Paul's letters (Galatians 6 verse 2). After a century in which much attention has been given to the revision of the services of the Church, liturgical usage would now lead a vicar to identify the gospel in a quotation from St Matthew:

'You shall love the Lord your God with all your heart, and with all your soul, and with all your mind.'
'You shall love your neighbour as yourself.'

Matthew 22 verses 37,39

Chapter Eight

Conclusion

The history of our community is important for our self-understanding. The early inhabitants of Darsham carved a precarious existence out of the forests and marshes of East Anglia, but this community survived, grew, changed and adapted. That resilience is still with us. Darsham is a place where we become aware of a common past, common feelings, and a common endeavour.

The parish church is the oldest continuing village organisation; as well as serving the village inhabitants it has been a link with strands of spirituality beyond the immediate environment. The fact that public worship has been maintained, as far as we can know, for a thousand years has a series of theological implications. Within Christian doctrine, the universal church understands its life as an extension through time of the Incarnation. The life of this church has represented the continuing presence of Christ in our community. Christ's standards of compassion and involvement are seen to evolve through ten centuries. Equally, the continuity of worship offered over a thousand years is a stepping stone from which our thoughts can move on to our share in the eternal worship of the everlasting God.

The reformation aimed to sanctify everyday life so that the whole of life can be offered to God. Towards the end of the millennium, the opportunities for worship have been diversified by the chapel. How fortunate we are that links between chapel and church have been so fruitful.

To conclude: there are three main continuities reflected in this book: place, migrant residents, and the presence of the Divine. The way that the local and the eternal are interwoven will enrich and challenge us for the future.

> 'But do not forget this one thing, dear friends: With the Lord a day is like a thousand years, and a thousand years are like a day.'
>
> *2 Peter 3 v 8*

THE AUTHORS

Olive Doris Reeve, nee Davidge, born 1929, received secondary education at the Green School for Girls, Isleworth, Middlesex where she excelled in maths, technical drawing and sport. Studied Engineering Drawing whilst employed at Gillette Industries and when qualified, worked for a number of national companies. She married in 1951 and had one son. She and her husband Ron moved to Suffolk in 1952 and when she retired, she researched the history of her parish of Darsham, building up a large archive of material which she used for local history exhibitions and as a source for the Darsham local history trilogy. Olive lived by a strong moral code that she learned from childhood. Her first priority was always to her family. She gave unconditional love and this was returned. She also had a wide circle of friends, both locally and also, because of her researches, worldwide, and she valued their friendship.

Richard Ginn, born 1951, received secondary education at Haberdashers' Aske's School at Elstree, Herts., and then worked in Banks in London for six years. He attended theological colleges in North London and Durham before ordination in 1979. He married Linda in 1980, and they have three children. Richard was vicar of Darsham and a number of parishes 1985 - 2013. He is a graduate of the Universities of London and Durham, as well as holding the Lambeth Diploma in Theology. In addition to helping with the Darsham trilogy, Richard is also the author of 'The Present and Past' (Pickwick Publications, 1989), 'The Labour of Love - William Burkitt and his Ministry at Dedham 1692-1703' (Dedham Ecclesiastical Lectureship Trust, 2003) 'The Politics of Prayer in Early Modern Britain' (Taurus Academic Studies, 2007) and various articles contributed to the Oxford Dictionary of National Biography. Richard and Linda have shared in the parishes where they served in building collaborative ministry and Parish Nursing. They have concluded that the only way in which the challenges of parish life can be tackled is with commitment and enthusiasm.